the splendid spoonful

the splendid spoonful

FROM **CUSTARD** TO **CRÈME BRÛLÉE**

by

BARBARA LAUTERBACH

photographs by

KIRSTEN STRECKER

CHRONICLE BOOKS

SAN FRANCISCO

dedication

To Richard Ressler – A Gentle Man
With gratitude and thanks, for the idea for this book

Library of Congress Cataloging-in-Publication Data available.

ISBN-13: 978-0-8118-4502-1
ISBN-10: 0-8118-4502-8

Manufactured in China.

Prop styling by **CINDY DiPRIMA**
Food styling by **TONI BROGAN**
Designed by **SUGAR**

Distributed in Canada by Raincoast Books
9050 Shaughnessy Street
Vancouver, British Columbia V6P 6E5

10 9 8 7 6 5 4 3 2

Chronicle Books LLC
85 Second Street
San Francisco, California 94105

www.chroniclebooks.com

acknowledgments

MY DEEPEST AND SINCERE THANK YOU TO ALL WHO MADE THIS BOOK A REALITY

My Chronicle "family," Bill LeBlond and Amy Treadwell, for continued support and encouragement

The Board who saw beyond stodgy

Jan Hughes and Doug Ogan once again for careful editorial detail

Yolanda Accinelli for excellent production

Sugar for their wonderfully imaginative interpretation of the subject

Kirsten Strecker for her most luscious photography

Deborah Kops for her eagle-eye editing done with grace

Susan Ginsburg, my literary agent extraordinaire, for her enthusiasm and support

Praise and thanks for my knowledgeable recipe testers and tasters; Gwen Miller, Tom Wilson, Chuck DiCecca and Rob Ulman, Deanna Fritz, Wendy Van de Poll, Linda Huntress, Tuffy Hamblet, Marian Touhey, Marilyn Patenaude, Fran Secord, Denny Stringfellow, Barbara Cleary, and Nancy Curran

My amazing assistant, "Coach Liz" Lapham

Cindy Barnes for her gracious willingness to go out of her way for ingredients

Barbara Gulino for her wonderful imagination with titles

Center Harbor Town Office staff Sheila Mohan, Robin Woodaman, and Master Patrolman Robert Nedeau

contents

introduction

NOT YOUR MOTHER'S CUSTARD

THE WONDERFULLY RICH and creamy concoction known as custard has been enjoyed since medieval days, and has evolved through many mutations of a simple principle: the mixture of eggs and sweetened milk, warmed together. Guinevere no doubt tempted Lancelot with a smooth Syllabub (page 102), just as today's cook would present a luscious Grand Marnier Crème Brûlée (page 52) to please family members or guests. Adding custard to your cooking repertoire can be both easy and rewarding. There are only a couple of basic techniques to master, and once in hand, they can be applied to a whole range of sweet and savory dishes.

Although basic custard is often thought of as nursery or comfort food, it can be the basis for sophisticated dishes, such as Tiramisu Cortonese (page 96). This book includes preparations made on top of the stove and in the oven. Most of the recipes can be made in advance, which is always a boon for today's multitasking cook, and will appeal to young and old alike.

Some recipes are departure points for others. Think of custard sauce, and then its application to the all-time favorite, floating islands (page 89), or a multilayered trifle (page 99) resplendent in a sparkling glass bowl. When custard becomes crème anglaise, a bowl of tiny fraises des bois can be napped with it or it can become a velvety underpinning for a slice of moist, dark chocolate cake.

I have also included custard-based recipes from other countries, such as a luscious French clafouti (pages 91 and 93) and a sublimely creamy Italian zabaglione (page 94).

Custard need not be limited to the sweet end of the meal. Savory custards make elegant side dishes or appetizers, such as Spinach-Parmesan Timbales (page 27) in a pool of tomato sauce, or the elegant Truffle Custard with Cabernet Sauce (page 26). Attention is also given to seasonal adaptations, such as tart-sweet Cranberry-Mascarpone Pots de Crème (page 76) and tender Raisin-Eggnog Bread Pudding (page 48).

Although not difficult to prepare, custard can be temperamental if not properly handled. You will find some simple tips in the next chapter so you can avoid the pitfalls of making custard.

As an experienced cooking teacher, I have noticed that whenever a custard-based dessert is on the class menu, it becomes the most popular dish of the day. The students master the simple technique very quickly, and return to it time and again to enjoy the praise they receive from family and friends, who are impressed with their skill. The variations on custard-based creations is endless, and the appeal, universal.

chapter 1: the basics

what's in a name?

All crèmes brûlées are custard, but not every custard is a crème brûlée. The following explanation will help you understand the many manifestations of custard. The first four have French names, which gives you some idea of custard's importance in French kitchens.

CRÈME BRÛLÉE (or "burnt cream") is a cooked and chilled custard that is sprinkled with brown or granulated sugar just before serving, and run under a broiler. According to James Beard it originated in England, where a seventeenth-century cookery book refers to it as "grilled cream." A torch especially made for this task may be used instead of a broiler. The sugar becomes brittle and crunchy, creating a delicious contrast to the silken custard beneath.

POT DE CRÈME (or "pot of cream") is a velvety smooth custard traditionally baked and served in tiny porcelain custard cups with lids, although any small ramekin may be used. The traditional flavors are vanilla, chocolate, and coffee.

CRÈME CARAMEL (or "caramel cream") is also known as *crème renversée* ("reverse cream") because the custard is baked in a caramel-lined mold, chilled for at least three hours, and then inverted for serving, so that the caramel forms a glaze on the top. In Mediterranean and Latin countries it is known as flan.

CRÈME ANGLAISE is a stirred, cooked custard sauce, which can be served warm or chilled. It is spooned over fruit, cake, or pastry, or eaten as a pastry filling. The sauce is used in both English trifle and Italian zuppa inglese, rich desserts that include cake, fresh or candied fruit, and sometimes whipped cream as well.

BREAD PUDDINGS are made with bread, milk or cream, eggs, and a variety of ingredients, either sweet or savory. Many bread puddings are best when made ahead of time and refrigerated until you are ready to bake. For this reason, savory bread puddings and stratas are ideal fare for celebratory breakfasts or brunches. The word *strata* comes from the Italian, meaning "layers." A strata is essentially a savory bread pudding in which the ingredients are layered. It is generally assembled the day before serving.

what makes custard come together?

If you understand how the ingredients interact when you make any custard-based preparation, from crème brûlée to bread pudding, you will avoid the pitfalls and have delicious results. The question I am most frequently asked is "Why does my custard weep?" Keep reading!

The ingredients you are dealing with include eggs, milk, half-and-half or cream, sugar, a bit of salt, and various flavorings. These are combined and cooked on top of the stove, preferably in a double boiler, until thickened, and then chilled, or they are slowly baked in the oven in custard cups or ramekins (generally in a water bath) until barely firm. Generally, 1 whole large egg or 2 large egg yolks plus 2 tablespoons of sugar will thicken 1 cup of milk or cream. These are minimum proportions; more eggs and sugar may be called for, depending on the recipe.

Heavy cream and whipping cream are interchangeable in the recipes in this book, as are light cream and half-and-half. If you can find cream that has not been ultra-pasteurized, by all means use it. Some recipes will call for light cream or milk. The fat content of the liquid affects the time that it takes the dish to "set up." A mixture with a higher fat content will set up more quickly. Custard-based preparations should be creamy and silky to the tongue, never curdled or runny. The mixture thickens because the proteins released by the egg jell when heated. If the custard is cooked rapidly or at too high a temperature, curdling will occur as the proteins jell too quickly, forming clumps.

If you are making a stirred custard (as opposed to an oven-baked custard), constant stirring over low heat will prevent the proteins from forming curds. Cooking custard in a saucepan over direct heat can be tricky. Most cooks prefer to make custard in the top of a double boiler—a pan of simmering water with an insert pan on top—because the bottom of the insert comes in contact with the steam from the hot water, not the burner itself. You can place a saucepan over a slightly larger pan of simmering water for the same effect. Custards will start to thicken when they reach about 150°F, and should be done at 180°F. To test for doneness, run your finger over the back of the stirring spoon; it should leave a clear track. The custard will thicken as it cools. Slow heat and patience will ensure success. If you do see little bits of lumpy egg in the mixture after cooking, strain the custard through a wire mesh sieve, or you can blitz it in a blender. Lightly buttering or spraying the ramekin or baking dish with vegetable-oil cooking spray ensures that none of the cooked custard will adhere to the dish. This step is essential if you are unmolding the custard.

Oven custards are cooked in a moderate oven in a hot water bath or bain-marie, a pan filled with hot water that comes partway up the sides of the custard-filled ramekins or custard cups. I find that a roasting pan with handles works well. A dish towel, folded to fit and placed in the bottom of the pan before the ramekins are added, prevents the bottoms from getting too hot and keeps them from slipping around when you pull the pan out of the oven. (Make sure the towel is not hanging over the edge of the pan, or it will "wick," or suck, the water out of the pan and release it onto the floor of the oven.) To make a bain-marie, place the custard cups or ramekins in a roasting pan, and fill them. Put the pan on the oven rack in a preheated oven, and then carefully add enough hot water (I pour it from a tea kettle) to come halfway up the sides of the cups. The hot water protects the custards from direct heat. To check for doneness, insert a knife close (about ½ inch) to the edge. It should come out clean. Or, while the custard is still wobbly in the center, touch the surface; the custard is ready if your finger comes away clean. The most common error beginners make is to leave the custard in the oven too long. The custard will continue to cook as it cools. Overcooking will produce watery or "weeping" custard. As home ovens are generally off by about 25°F one way or the other, it's a good idea to check your oven with an oven thermometer.

Some recipes will instruct you to scald the milk or cream. This method was generally used in former times to keep milk from souring. To scald milk or cream, heat it to just below the boil, or until you see steam rising from the edges of the pan.

useful cookware

DOUBLE BOILER: A saucepan with an insert pan. One lid fits both pans. Water is poured into the lower pan and brought to a simmer; the custard mixture or other heat-sensitive food cooks in the upper pan. The simmering water in the lower pan provides indirect heat and helps keep the custard mixture at a low, even temperature.

WATER BATH OR BAIN-MARIE: A single container or individual ones are set in a larger shallow pan partially filled with hot water, which provides low, indirect heat during baking.

PROPANE OR BUTANE TORCH: A small blowtorch designed for cooking, available in kitchenware stores. Look for a refillable torch with a fuel gauge. Some torches have adjustable flames, which is helpful. An extra canister of fuel is a good investment.

CUSTARD CUPS: Individual Pyrex or earthenware ovenproof cups, slightly wider at the top than at the base, usually with a 6- or 8-ounce capacity.

POTS DE CRÈME CUPS: Small ceramic ovenproof cups with lids, which are used for custards. The lid keeps a skin from forming on the custard.

RAMEKINS: Small ceramic ovenproof dishes with straight sides that resemble soufflé dishes and have a 4- to 6-ounce capacity. Ramekins are also available with low sides. These generally have a 4-ounce capacity.

NOTE: Custard cups, ramekins, and any other small ovenproof baking containers are interchangeable for the recipes in this book. Just adjust the size of each serving to the container you have on hand. If you have four 6-ounce containers, and the recipe calls for six 4-ounce containers, you will have 4 larger servings. Be aware, however, that if you substitute other containers that are much larger or smaller than the recommended size, the cooking time will be affected. Crèmes and custards will set up a bit faster in shallow containers.

chapter 2: the savory side

turkey day butternut custard

ALTHOUGH THANKSGIVING menus across the country are generally written in stone, occasionally it's fun to throw something different into the mix. This delicious treatment of butternut squash will certainly bring kudos for the cook. You could unmold the ramekins and serve all the custards on a platter, or serve one ramekin to each person.

PLACE THE OVEN RACK in the middle position and preheat the oven to 325°F. Butter or spray the ramekins.

IN A MEDIUM SAUCEPAN, whisk together the cream, milk, syrup, and pureed squash. Heat just until barely simmering.

IN A MEDIUM BOWL, whisk together the egg yolks, cinnamon, nutmeg, salt, and pepper.

POUR THE SQUASH MIXTURE very slowly into the yolks, whisking constantly. Pour the custard through a fine-mesh sieve into a large measuring cup, pressing the liquid out of the solids. Place the prepared ramekins in a baking pan lined with a dish towel.

POUR THE STRAINED MIXTURE into the ramekins. Set the pan on the oven rack. Carefully add enough hot water to come halfway up the sides of the ramekins.

BAKE THE CUSTARDS for 35 to 40 minutes, or until set and a knife inserted near the edge comes out clean. Serve the custards immediately, or hold, covered, for up to 30 minutes.

ingredients

	SOFTENED BUTTER OR VEGETABLE-OIL COOKING SPRAY FOR THE RAMEKINS
1	CUP HEAVY CREAM
3/4	CUP MILK
1/2	CUP PURE MAPLE SYRUP
1/2	CUP COOKED AND PUREED BUTTERNUT SQUASH (USE A FOOD PROCESSOR OR BLENDER)
6	LARGE EGG YOLKS
1/4	TEASPOON GROUND CINNAMON
1/8	TEASPOON FRESHLY GRATED NUTMEG
1/4	TEASPOON SALT
	FRESHLY GROUND BLACK PEPPER TO TASTE
6	4-OUNCE RAMEKINS

ingredients

2	TEASPOONS UNSALTED BUTTER PLUS SOFTENED BUTTER OR VEGETABLE-OIL COOKING SPRAY FOR THE RAMEKINS
2	CUPS HALF-AND-HALF
2	SHALLOTS, FINELY CHOPPED
6	LARGE EGG YOLKS
1/2	TEASPOON SALT
	FRESHLY GROUND BLACK PEPPER TO TASTE
1	CUP LOOSELY PACKED WHITE CRABMEAT, FLAKED
6	4-OUNCE RAMEKINS

{ingredients continued}

*serves 6

crabmeat custard with herbed beurre blanc

WHEN I FIRST MADE this elegant dish for friends it received rave reviews. If served for brunch or as a first course it is particularly attractive if you unmold the ramekins onto individual plates and drizzle them with the herbed beurre blanc, a classic French butter sauce. I like to make it with luscious fresh crabmeat from Maine. You can find fresh or frozen crabmeat in most seafood stores and the seafood sections of supermarkets. A high-quality canned crabmeat would work, too.

PLACE THE OVEN RACK in the middle position and preheat the oven to 325°F. Butter or spray the ramekins.

IN A SMALL SAUCEPAN, heat the half-and-half just until steam rises from the pan. Remove from the heat.

IN A SMALL SKILLET, melt the 2 teaspoons of butter and briefly sauté the shallots, just until limp. Remove from the heat.

IN A MEDIUM BOWL, whisk the egg yolks until slightly thickened; add the salt, pepper, and sautéed shallots. Add the flaked crabmeat and stir to combine. Slowly add the warm half-and-half and stir again gently to combine.

PLACE THE PREPARED RAMEKINS in a baking pan lined with a dish towel. Ladle the cream and crab mixture into the ramekins, distributing the crabmeat evenly. Place the baking pan on the oven rack. Carefully add enough hot water to come halfway up the sides of the ramekins.

{continued}

ingredients

✳ herbed beurre blanc

1/3 CUP WHITE WINE VINEGAR

1/3 CUP DRY VERMOUTH

3 TABLESPOONS MINCED SHALLOTS

  SALT AND FRESHLY GROUND BLACK PEPPER TO TASTE

3/4 CUP (1½ STICKS) COLD UNSALTED BUTTER, CUT INTO PIECES

2 TABLESPOONS MINCED FRESH CHIVES

2 TABLESPOONS MINCED FRESH CURLY PARSLEY

6 4-OUNCE RAMEKINS

crabmeat custard with herbed beurre blanc {continued}

BAKE THE CUSTARDS for 30 to 35 minutes, or until set and a knife inserted near the edge comes out clean.

MEANWHILE, MAKE THE BEURRE BLANC: In a heavy, medium-sized saucepan over high heat, combine the vinegar, vermouth, shallots, salt, and pepper and boil until reduced to no more than ¼ cup. (The sauce may be set aside at this point until the ramekins are almost ready to serve.) Just before serving, return the pan to a very low heat. Add the butter, piece by piece, whisking constantly until it is all incorporated. Stop the minute the sauce is smooth and creamy. Add the chives and parsley.

REMOVE THE PAN with the ramekins from the oven. With a dish towel, carefully remove the ramekins from the water bath. Unmold them onto individual plates and spoon the herbed beurre blanc sauce over each one. Serve at once.

ingredients

SOFTENED BUTTER OR VEGETABLE-OIL COOKING SPRAY FOR THE RAMEKINS

6 LARGE EGGS

2 TEASPOONS FINELY CHOPPED PARSLEY, PLUS EXTRA FOR GARNISH

2 TEASPOONS MINCED ONION

1/8 TEASPOON FRESHLY GROUND BLACK PEPPER

1/4 TEASPOON SALT

1 CUP HALF-AND-HALF

2 TOMATOES, DICED, FOR GARNISH

6 4-OUNCE RAMEKINS

*serves 6

breakfast custard omelets

CUSTARD FOR BREAKFAST? WHY NOT? During my days as an innkeeper, coming up with a variety of delicious breakfasts for guests who stayed more than two or three nights was a challenge. After I'd gone through my repertoire of frittatas, French toast, pancakes, waffles, and the like, I would sometimes make these individual custard "omelets"; the ingredients were dictated by what I had on hand. To the basic recipe, I would add a little chopped ham, bacon or sausage, or finely chopped peppers, cooked mushrooms, or tomatoes. Almost anything goes, as long as it's well drained and patted dry. Think about what you like in an omelet and take it from there!

PLACE AN OVEN RACK in the middle position and preheat the oven to 325°F. Butter or spray the ramekins.

IN A MEDIUM BOWL, whisk the eggs until slightly thickened. Add the parsley, onion, pepper, salt, and half-and-half. Whisk until combined.

PLACE THE PREPARED RAMEKINS in a baking pan lined with a dish towel. Ladle the egg mixture into the ramekins. Place the baking pan on the oven rack and carefully add enough hot water to come halfway up the sides of the ramekins.

COVER THE RAMEKINS with a sheet of foil and bake for 30 minutes, or until set and a knife inserted near the edge comes out clean. Carefully remove the ramekins from the water bath with a dish towel. Serve the omelets in the ramekins, or unmold onto individual plates. Serve at once, garnished with the diced tomato and parsley.

*serves 8

curried corn custard

WHEN FRESH CORN SEASON ARRIVES, I can't get enough of it. I eat it every night, usually dripping in sweet butter with a dash of salt. However, delicately flavored corn custard is a nice change of pace if you are entertaining. You can bake this custard in a single baking dish, or for a more elegant presentation, divide it among individual ramekins.

PLACE THE OVEN RACK in the middle position and preheat the oven to 350°F. Spray a 12-x-8-inch baking dish with the cooking spray.

IN A LARGE BOWL, combine the corn with the eggs. Stir in the flour, sugar, curry powder, salt, and pepper. Add 2 tablespoons of the melted butter and all of the cream. Mix well. Pour the custard into the prepared baking dish.

AT THIS POINT, the dish may be covered with plastic wrap and refrigerated for up to 3 hours. If refrigerating, bring to room temperature 30 minutes before baking.

PLACE THE CUSTARD in the oven and bake for 35 minutes.

MEANWHILE, combine the cracker crumbs with the thyme and the remaining 2 tablespoons of butter. Sprinkle the mixture over the custard. Bake for 10 minutes longer or until the custard is set and a knife inserted near the edge comes out clean. Garnish with the chopped parsley and serve immediately.

ingredients

VEGETABLE OIL-COOKING SPRAY FOR THE BAKING DISH

3 CUPS FRESH CORN KERNELS (5 TO 6 EARS), OR FROZEN CORN, THAWED

3 LARGE EGGS, BEATEN

1/4 CUP ALL-PURPOSE FLOUR

1 TABLESPOON LIGHT BROWN SUGAR

1 1/2 TEASPOONS CURRY POWDER

3/4 TEASPOON SALT

1/4 TEASPOON FRESHLY GROUND WHITE PEPPER

4 TABLESPOONS UNSALTED BUTTER, MELTED

2 CUPS LIGHT CREAM

1 CUP SALTED CRACKER CRUMBS

1/4 TEASPOON DRIED THYME

CHOPPED FRESH CURLY PARSLEY FOR GARNISH

ingredients

4 TABLESPOONS UNSALTED BUTTER PLUS SOFTENED BUTTER OR VEGETABLE-OIL COOKING SPRAY FOR THE RAMEKINS

2 CUPS SLICED SHALLOTS (ABOUT 8 MEDIUM SHALLOTS)

3 LARGE EGGS

1/4 TEASPOON SALT

1/4 TEASPOON FRESHLY GROUND WHITE PEPPER

1 TEASPOON BAKING POWDER

1 CUP HEAVY CREAM

1/2 CUP FRESHLY GRATED PARMESAN CHEESE

4 6-OUNCE RAMEKINS OR ONE 1-QUART BAKING DISH

serves 4

shallot custard

A MEMBER OF THE onion family, the shallot is prized by French cooks for its subtle, sweet taste. It is the barely perceptible undertone in the piquant flavor of béarnaise sauce as well as beurre blanc. The shallot, which is becoming more readily available in this country, lends its unique flavor to this simple but elegant custard, a perfect accompaniment to grilled meats or a roast. My cooking classes gave this custard an A-plus. Look for shallots sold in bulk rather than those packed two to a box, because the latter tend to be older and drier.

PLACE THE OVEN RACK in the middle position and preheat the oven to 350°F. Lightly butter or spray the ramekins or baking dish.

IN A HEAVY SKILLET, melt the butter over medium heat. Add the shallots and sauté, stirring, until they are nicely browned. Set aside.

IN A MEDIUM BOWL, lightly whisk the eggs with the salt, pepper, and baking powder. Stir in the cream and the grated Parmesan. Fold in the shallots. Set the prepared ramekins or baking dish in a large baking pan lined with a dish towel. Ladle the mixture into the ramekins or baking dish and place the pan on the oven rack.

BAKE THE CUSTARD for about 30 minutes for the ramekins, and 35 to 40 minutes for the baking dish, or until firm to the touch and slightly browned. Remove from the oven and serve at once.

ingredients

VEGETABLE-OIL COOKING SPRAY FOR THE RAMEKINS

1 CUP HEAVY CREAM

3/4 CUP MILK

2 CLOVES GARLIC, PEELED

1 TEASPOON SALT

1/2 TEASPOON FRESHLY GROUND WHITE PEPPER

1 10-OUNCE PACKAGE FROZEN ARTICHOKE HEARTS

1/2 CUP ASPARAGUS TIPS, PLUS 18 TIPS FOR GARNISH (ABOUT 1 1/2 POUNDS SLENDER ASPARAGUS; RESERVE THE STALKS FOR ANOTHER USE)

2 LARGE EGGS

2 LARGE EGG YOLKS

1/4 CUP FRESHLY GRATED GRUYÈRE CHEESE

6 FOUR-OUNCE RAMEKINS

*serves 6

asparagus and artichoke flans

THESE DELICATE, PALE-GREEN FLANS, were inspired by a recipe from my amazing friend Lora Brody's beautiful cookbook *The Cape Cod Table*. Here's my version, with a tip of the toque to Lora.

LIGHTLY SPRAY the ramekins with cooking spray.

IN A MEDIUM SAUCEPAN, combine the cream, milk, garlic, salt, and pepper and heat over medium heat just until steam rises around the edges of the liquid. Set aside to cool.

COOK THE ARTICHOKE HEARTS according to the directions on the package. Chop coarsely and set aside. In a small saucepan, cook the asparagus tips in boiling water over high heat just until tender, about 3 to 4 minutes. Drain and set aside.

PLACE THE OVEN RACK in the middle position and preheat the oven to 325°F.

POUR THE COOLED CREAM mixture into a blender or a food processor. Add the artichokes and asparagus. Blend or process briefly, then add the eggs, egg yolks, and cheese and puree until smooth.

PLACE THE PREPARED RAMEKINS in a baking pan lined with a dish towel. Ladle the mixture into the ramekins. Place the pan on the oven rack and pour enough hot water into the pan to come halfway up the sides of the ramekins.

BAKE THE FLANS for 30 to 35 minutes, or until set and a knife inserted near the edge comes out clean.

serves 4

truffle custard with cabernet sauce

IF YOU ARE ENTERTAINING and want to pull out all the stops, prepare these tiny, delicate, truffle oil-infused custards as a first course or appetizer. Exquisitely scented fungi, truffles, and truffle oil can be found in specialty food shops. This savory recipe is the creation of Linda Stradley, cookbook author, food historian, and television personality.

PLACE THE OVEN RACK in the middle position and preheat the oven to 325°F. Lightly butter the ramekins.

IN A SMALL SAUCEPAN, heat the milk just until steam begins to rise.

IN A LARGE BOWL, beat the egg and egg yolks lightly with a fork; add the salt and the white truffle oil. Slowly stir in the hot milk until blended. Place the prepared ramekins in a baking pan lined with a dish towel. Ladle the egg mixture into the ramekins. Set the pan on the oven rack. Carefully pour enough hot water into the pan to come halfway up the sides of the ramekins.

BAKE THE CUSTARDS for 10 to 15 minutes, or until set and a knife inserted near the edge comes out clean. Remove from the oven and immediately remove the ramekins from the water bath with a dish towel.

WHILE THE CUSTARDS ARE BAKING, reduce the beef stock until it is syrupy, about 6 minutes. Add the wine and stir to combine.

TO SERVE, place the warm custards on individual plates. Top each one with truffle shavings and drizzle with 1 to 2 teaspoons of the warm wine sauce. Serve immediately.

ingredients

SOFTENED BUTTER FOR THE RAMEKINS

3/4 CUP MILK

1 LARGE EGG

3 LARGE EGG YOLKS

1/8 TEASPOON SALT

1 TEASPOON WHITE TRUFFLE OIL

1 CUP GOOD-QUALITY BEEF STOCK

1-2 TABLESPOONS CABERNET WINE

BLACK TRUFFLE SHAVINGS FOR GARNISH

4 4-OUNCE RAMEKINS

ingredients

✳ timbales

1	TABLESPOON UNSALTED BUTTER PLUS SOFTENED BUTTER OR VEGETABLE-OIL COOKING SPRAY FOR THE RAMEKINS
2	10-OUNCE PACKAGES FROZEN CHOPPED SPINACH, OR 2 POUNDS FRESH SPINACH, TRIMMED AND WELL WASHED
1/4	CUP FINELY CHOPPED SHALLOTS
3	LARGE EGGS
1 1/4	CUPS HALF-AND-HALF
3/4	CUP FRESHLY GRATED PARMESAN CHEESE
1	TEASPOON SALT
1/4	TEASPOON FRESHLY GRATED BLACK PEPPER
1/2	TEASPOON FRESHLY GRATED NUTMEG
8	4-OUNCE RAMEKINS

{ingredients continued}

spinach-parmesan timbales with tomato-basil coulis

A TIMBALE IS a molded, custard-based dish made with vegetables, seafood, or meat. "Timbale" is derived from the French word for drum, and refers to the cylindrical shape of the finished dish. I like to serve this spinach timbale as a first course, or as an accompaniment to grilled fish, or perhaps roast lamb. The brilliant green of the spinach is enhanced by a pool of lustrous red tomato coulis. If you only have time to make the timbales, they are delicious on their own. They may be served chilled, or can be made ahead, refrigerated, and reheated, a boon to the busy cook.

✳

PLACE THE OVEN RACK in the middle position and preheat the oven to 350°F. Lightly butter or spray the ramekins.

COOK THE FROZEN SPINACH according to the package directions for 1 to 3 minutes, and drain well. Or cook the fresh spinach in a large pot of boiling water until tender, about 1 minute. Drain and chop. You should have about 2 cups of chopped spinach.

IN A SMALL SKILLET, melt the tablespoon of butter and sauté the shallots until soft.

IN A LARGE BOWL, beat the eggs lightly, and stir in the spinach, shallots, half-and-half, cheese, salt, pepper, and nutmeg. Mix well to combine.

{continued}

ingredients

* **tomato-basil coulis**

(makes about 1½ cups)

2	TABLESPOONS OLIVE OIL
1/2	CUP FINELY CHOPPED ONIONS
2	CUPS ITALIAN PLUM TOMATOES, COARSELY CHOPPED, WITH THEIR JUICES
3	TABLESPOONS TOMATO PASTE
1	TABLESPOON FINELY CHOPPED FRESH BASIL
1	TEASPOON BROWN SUGAR
1/2	TEASPOON SALT
	FRESHLY GROUND BLACK PEPPER

spinach-parmesan timbales with tomato-basil coulis {continued}

LADLE THE SPINACH mixture into the prepared ramekins. Set the ramekins in a baking pan lined with a dish towel. Set the pan on the oven rack and carefully pour enough hot water into the baking pan to come halfway up the sides of the ramekins.

BAKE THE TIMBALES for 25 to 30 minutes, or just until set and a knife inserted near the edge comes out clean.

MEANWHILE, MAKE THE COULIS: In a 2- to 3-quart enameled or stainless steel saucepan, heat the olive oil over medium heat until a light haze forms. Add the onions and cook for 7 to 8 minutes, or until they are soft but not browned. Add the tomatoes, tomato paste, basil, sugar, salt, and a few grinds of pepper. Reduce the heat to very low and simmer, with the pan partially covered, for about 40 minutes, or until thick and bubbly. Stir occasionally.

IF DESIRED, press the sauce through a fine sieve (or food mill) into a bowl or a pan. Taste for seasoning and serve hot.

REMOVE THE PAN with the ramekins from the oven. With a dish towel, carefully remove the ramekins from the water bath and unmold onto a serving platter or individual plates. Pour the tomato coulis onto the large platter, or coat the surface of individual plates. Or serve the timbales in the ramekin without any sauce.

IF YOU WOULD LIKE to make this ahead, refrigerate until almost ready to serve. To reheat the ramekins, cover loosely with foil and place in a preheated 275°F oven for 15 minutes.

1	CUP ALL-PURPOSE FLOUR
1/2	TEASPOON SALT
2	LARGE EGGS, LIGHTLY BEATEN
1 1/4	CUPS WHOLE MILK
	FRESHLY GROUND BLACK PEPPER
12	OUNCES LINK BREAKFAST SAUSAGES
2	TABLESPOONS CANOLA OIL
	WARM MAPLE SYRUP FOR SERVING (OPTIONAL)

*serves 6-8

toad in the hole

THIS CLASSIC ENGLISH DISH became a favorite of my family when we were living in Newcastle-upon-Tyne, England. The weather in that beautiful, rugged part of northeast England can be cold and damp, and this hearty dish of puffy, golden brown custard encasing the "toads" or sausages, warmed us on many occasions. British "bangers" contain more bread than American sausages. They may be difficult to find, but a breakfast link sausage works here just as well. Upon returning home, we often made it into an Anglo-American dish by serving it with pure maple syrup. This is hearty, satisfying nourishment for a blustery day.

TO MAKE THE BATTER, in a medium bowl, sift the flour and salt together. Make a well in the center and pour the eggs into the well. Stir in the milk in a slow, steady stream, beginning in the center and gradually working in all the flour from the sides. When the mixture is well blended, add the pepper to taste and strain through a sieve into a bowl or large measuring cup. Let rest for 30 minutes.

PLACE THE OVEN RACK in the middle position and preheat the oven to 475°F.

PRICK THE SAUSAGES with a fork, put them in a pan of simmering water for 3 or 4 minutes, and drain on paper towels. (Alternatively, if you are using British sausages, omit this step.)

ADD THE OIL to a 9-x-11-inch baking pan and put the pan in the preheated oven. When the fat is very hot but not smoking, place the sausages in the pan, and pour on the batter. Return to the oven and reduce the heat to 425°F.

BAKE THE CUSTARD for 25 to 30 minutes, or until puffy and brown. Cut into squares, including some "toads" in each portion, and serve immediately, with warm maple syrup if desired.

chapter 3: bread puddings— savory & sweet

THE SAVORY

THE SWEET

4	TABLESPOONS UNSALTED BUTTER
1	12-OUNCE ROLL SPICY SAUSAGE MEAT
6	CUPS ¾-INCH BREAD CUBES FROM A DAY-OLD COUNTRY-STYLE LOAF (ABOUT 12 SLICES, CRUSTS REMOVED)
1	JALAPEÑO PEPPER, SEEDED AND MINCED
1	CUP FROZEN CORN KERNELS, THAWED, OR CANNED KERNELS, DRAINED
1/4	CUP CHOPPED RED BELL PEPPER
2	CUPS SHREDDED MONTEREY JACK PEPPER CHEESE (ABOUT 8 OUNCES)
6	LARGE EGGS
2	CUPS MILK
1/2	TEASPOON SALT
	FRESHLY GROUND BLACK PEPPER

*serves 6-8

southwest sausage and jalapeño bread pudding

ONE OF THE PLUSES of owning a bed and breakfast is the opportunity to meet people from all around the country. B&B guests are generally gregarious, even in the morning, and sometimes this hostess found herself engaged in wonderful conversations, which generally focused on why I had started a B&B, how long had I done it, and then, my favorite topic, breakfast. Guests would often share family recipes, and that's how this tasty breakfast bread pudding came into my repertoire. You don't have to be an innkeeper to appreciate the advance preparation of this dish. A platter of sweet fresh pineapple, mango, and kiwi slices makes a colorful accompaniment.

———*

MELT THE BUTTER in a small pan, and pour it into a 9-x-13-inch baking dish, swirling it around to coat the dish with the butter.

IN A MEDIUM SKILLET, crumble the sausage and brown it over medium-high heat until no longer pink. Remove the meat with a slotted spoon and drain on paper towels.

LAYER HALF OF THE CUBED BREAD in the buttered dish and sprinkle with half of the jalapeño, corn kernels, and red bell pepper. Sprinkle with all of the sausage and layer half of the cheese on top. Repeat the layers (except for the sausage), ending with the cheese.

{continued}

southwest sausage and jalapeño bread pudding {continued}

IN A MEDIUM BOWL, whisk the eggs until thickened, then whisk in the milk. Season the mixture with the salt and pepper to taste. Pour the mixture over the contents of the baking dish. Cover the dish with plastic wrap and refrigerate overnight.

REMOVE THE PUDDING from the refrigerator at least 30 minutes before baking. While the dish is coming to room temperature, place the oven rack in the middle position and preheat the oven to 350°F.

REMOVE THE PLASTIC WRAP and bake the dish for 50 minutes to 1 hour, or until puffed and golden, and a knife inserted near the edge comes out clean. Let it rest for 10 minutes before serving.

ingredients

3 TABLESPOONS UNSALTED BUTTER PLUS SOFTENED BUTTER OR VEGETABLE OIL COOKING SPRAY FOR THE BAKING DISH

1/2 CUP DRIED MUSHROOMS SUCH AS PORCINI, CHANTERELLES, OR MORELS (½ OUNCE)

3/4 CUP BOILING WATER

1 POUND ASSORTED FRESH MUSHROOMS, SUCH AS BUTTONS, CRIMINI, SHIITAKES, AND OYSTERS, STEMMED AND THINLY SLICED

1 LARGE YELLOW ONION, CHOPPED

2 TABLESPOONS CHOPPED FRESH THYME, OR 2 TEASPOONS DRIED

5 LARGE EGGS

2 CUPS MILK

2 TEASPOONS WORCESTERSHIRE SAUCE

DASH OF TABASCO SAUCE

SALT AND FRESHLY GROUND BLACK PEPPER

6 CUPS ¾-INCH BREAD CUBES FROM A DAY-OLD COUNTRY-STYLE LOAF (ABOUT 12 SLICES, CRUSTS REMOVED)

2 CUPS GRATED GRUYÈRE CHEESE

CHOPPED FRESH PARSLEY FOR GARNISH

*serves 6-8

herbed mushroom bread pudding

MUSHROOM AFICIONADOS will love this dish. Here, fresh mushrooms combine with the earthy taste of the dried mushrooms to produce a richly flavored, savory meatless pudding, suitable as a side dish or a main event. Use whatever mushrooms are available to you. If you have access to fresh morels, by all means include them. Dried mushrooms are found in packets at most supermarkets. All you need to complete the meal is a crisp salad of field greens with a tangy dressing and perhaps a glass of a robust red wine.

LIGHTLY BUTTER or spray an 11-x-7-inch baking dish.

PUT THE DRIED MUSHROOMS in a small bowl, and pour the boiling water over them. Set aside until soft, about 10 minutes. Place a piece of paper towel in a sieve and drain the mushrooms over a small bowl, reserving the liquid. Rinse the mushrooms lightly and pat dry.

IN A LARGE SKILLET, melt the 3 tablespoons of butter over medium-high heat. Add the fresh mushrooms and the onion; sauté for 3 minutes, or until limp. Add the reconstituted dried mushrooms and continue sautéing until the mushrooms have given up their liquid and are nicely browned, about 10 to 12 minutes. Stir in the thyme and transfer the mushrooms to a bowl.

IN A LARGE BOWL, whisk together the eggs, milk, reserved mushroom liquid, Worcestershire sauce, Tabasco sauce, and salt and pepper to taste until well blended.

{continued}

herbed mushroom bread pudding {continued}

ARRANGE HALF OF THE BREAD CUBES over the bottom of the prepared baking dish. Top with the mushroom mixture and then layer with half of the cheese, then the remaining bread cubes, and the rest of the cheese. Using a ladle, gently pour the egg and milk mixture over the bread and mushroom mixture, being careful to cover all the bread cubes with the liquid. Press the bread cubes gently with the palm of your hand or the back of a spatula to immerse them if necessary. At this point you may cover the pudding with plastic wrap and refrigerate for several hours, or even overnight.

WHEN READY TO BAKE, remove the pudding from the refrigerator and allow it to come to room temperature.

PLACE THE OVEN RACK in the middle position and preheat the oven to 350°F. Bake the pudding until it is puffy and golden brown, or until a knife inserted near the edge comes out clean, about 40 minutes.

GARNISH WITH PARSLEY and serve immediately.

ingredients

6 CUPS ¾-INCH BREAD CUBES FROM A DAY-OLD COUNTRY-STYLE LOAF (ABOUT 12 SLICES, CRUSTS REMOVED)

3/4 CUP MELTED BUTTER

4 CUPS WATER

1 1/2 CUPS DICED CARROTS

2 1/2 CUPS COARSELY CHOPPED BROCCOLI (FLORETS AND STEMS)

SOFTENED BUTTER OR VEGETABLE-OIL COOKING SPRAY FOR THE BAKING DISH

2 CUPS SHREDDED EXTRA-SHARP CHEDDAR CHEESE (8 OUNCES)

4 LARGE EGGS

2 CUPS MILK

GENEROUS DASH OF TABASCO SAUCE

1 TEASPOON SALT

1/2 TEASPOON FRESHLY GROUND BLACK PEPPER

*serves 6-8

watch hill veggie-cheese breakfast strata

ON MANY OCCASIONS at my bed and breakfast, Watch Hill, I would have vegetarian guests. With a little notice I made this versatile dish the night before. You may vary the vegetables and type of cheese. Be creative, but make sure the quantity of vegetables does not exceed 4 cups.

❋

IN A MEDIUM BOWL, toss the bread cubes with the melted butter and set aside.

IN A MEDIUM SAUCEPAN, bring the water to a boil and cook the carrots briefly, until barely tender, about 3 to 4 minutes. Remove them with a slotted spoon and drain well in a colander. Add the broccoli to the boiling water and cook very briefly, no more than a minute. Drain well, wrap in paper towels, and squeeze to remove all moisture.

BUTTER OR SPRAY a 9-x-13-inch baking dish. Layer the ingredients, starting with half of the bread cubes and adding half of the shredded cheese, all of the carrots, all of the broccoli, the remaining bread cubes, and the remaining cheese.

IN A MEDIUM BOWL, whisk together the eggs and milk thoroughly and add the seasonings.

POUR THE MIXTURE evenly over the ingredients in the baking dish. Cover with plastic wrap and refrigerate for at least 2 hours, or overnight.

PLACE THE OVEN RACK in the middle position and preheat the oven to 350°F. Remove the strata from the refrigerator 30 minutes prior to baking. Bake until puffy and nicely browned, or until a knife inserted near the edge comes out clean, about 35 to 40 minutes. Serve immediately.

serves 8

watch hill brie strata with fruit salsa

IF I HAD TO PICK A FAVORITE recipe from this collection, this might be it. When I owned Watch Hill Bed and Breakfast, I was featured on the local TV channel preparing this signature dish. Perfect for elegant entertaining, it is easy to put together the night before. The tart Fruit Salsa is the perfect accompaniment. A platter of spiral-cut ham slices complements the rich flavor of the Brie.

———————●——

PUT THE OVEN RACK in the middle position and preheat the oven to 350°F. Butter or spray a 9-x-13-inch baking dish.

BUTTER ONE SIDE of each of the bread slices.

IN A MEDIUM BOWL, whisk the eggs until blended and then whisk in the milk and salt. Cut the Brie into ½-inch cubes.

PLACE HALF THE BREAD SLICES, buttered side up, in the prepared baking dish. Top with half the Brie cubes. Repeat with the remaining bread and Brie. Pour the milk and egg mixture over the bread. Sprinkle the strata with paprika. Let stand for 30 minutes before baking, or cover with plastic wrap and refrigerate overnight. (If refrigerating overnight, remove the strata from the refrigerator 30 minutes before baking.)

PLACE THE BAKING DISH in the oven and bake for 35 to 40 minutes, until nicely browned and puffy. It will soon fall like a soufflé, but do not be concerned. To serve, cut the strata into squares and serve with the Fruit Salsa alongside.

MAKE THE FRUIT SALSA: combine all the ingredients in a glass serving bowl. Refrigerate for up to 2 hours, or serve immediately with the strata.

ingredients

4-5 TABLESPOONS BUTTER, SOFTENED, PLUS EXTRA SOFTENED BUTTER OR VEGETABLE-OIL COOKING SPRAY FOR THE PAN

8-10 SLICES FIRM WHITE BREAD (CRUSTS REMOVED)

4 LARGE EGGS

1½ CUPS MILK

1 TEASPOON SALT

1 POUND BRIE, CHILLED AND RIND REMOVED

  PINCH OF PAPRIKA

✳ fruit salsa

1 PINT FRESH STRAWBERRIES, HULLED AND DICED

1 ANJOU PEAR, CORED AND DICED

1 RED APPLE, CORED AND DICED

1 TABLESPOON HONEY

1 TABLESPOON FRESH LIME JUICE

* serves 6-8

anne's french toast crème brûlée

THIS IS THE BEST of all worlds, the flavors of crème brûlée and French toast combined in one scrumptious recipe. Elegant enough for a very special brunch, it would be perfect for Christmas morning as well. The recipe was created by Anne McNeill, whom I met at an alumnae conference at Smith College. Anne is a Californian, and I'm a New Englander, but we soon discovered that we were both "foodies" and had both run bed and breakfasts. This led to trading recipes, of course. I think I benefited most in this swap! Preparing the dish the night before is a bonus to the busy cook. Anne says for an especially decadent dish, substitute slightly stale croissants or challah bread for the baguette.

———⊛———

BUTTER OR LIGHTLY SPRAY a 9-x-13-inch baking dish.

IN A SMALL SAUCEPAN combine the corn syrup, maple syrup, butter, and brown sugar and simmer over medium heat, stirring, until smooth. Pour the mixture into the prepared baking pan. Place the bread slices in one layer in the syrup mixture.

IN A LARGE BOWL, whisk together the eggs, half-and-half, vanilla, Grand Marnier (if using), orange zest, and salt. Pour evenly over the bread. Cover with plastic wrap and refrigerate overnight.

THE NEXT DAY, place the oven rack in the middle position and preheat the oven to 350°F. While the oven preheats, bring the baking dish to room temperature.

BAKE THE FRENCH TOAST for 45 minutes, or until puffy and golden. Cut into squares and serve immediately with additional maple syrup, or a dollop of sour cream or crème fraîche.

ingredients

SOFTENED BUTTER OR VEGETABLE-OIL COOKING SPRAY FOR THE BAKING DISH

1 TABLESPOON LIGHT CORN SYRUP

1 TABLESPOON MAPLE SYRUP

1/2 CUP (1 STICK) BUTTER

1 CUP FIRMLY PACKED LIGHT BROWN SUGAR

1 BAGUETTE, SLICED INTO 1-INCH-THICK SLICES

6 LARGE EGGS

2 CUPS HALF-AND-HALF

2 TEASPOONS VANILLA EXTRACT

2 TEASPOONS GRAND MARNIER (OPTIONAL)

GRATED ZEST OF 1 LARGE ORANGE

1/4 TEASPOON SALT

ADDITIONAL MAPLE SYRUP, OR SOUR CREAM OR CRÈME FRAÎCHE FOR SERVING (OPTIONAL)

SOFTENED BUTTER OR VEGETABLE-OIL
COOKING SPRAY FOR THE BAKING DISH

serves 8-10

spiced bread pudding with tuffy's bourbon sauce

HERE IS THE ULTIMATE comfort food. There will be many a Dickensian "More please?" when you serve this luscious dessert, slightly warm, accompanied by a spoonful of my friend Tuffy Hamblet's bourbon sauce.

— ⋯⋯⊛⋯ —

PLACE THE OVEN RACK in the middle position and preheat the oven to 350°F.

BUTTER OR SPRAY a 9 x-13 inch baking dish. Put the torn bread chunks in a large bowl.

IN A MEDIUM BOWL, whisk the eggs until well blended, and then stir in the milk, melted butter, sugar, vanilla, cinnamon, ginger, and nutmeg. (The spices will be visible.)

POUR THE EGG MIXTURE over the bread chunks and mix gently with a wooden spoon. The mixture should be moist, but not soupy. Pour the mixture into the prepared baking pan. Bake the pudding for 1 hour, or until the top is golden brown and puffy.

MEANWHILE, MAKE THE SAUCE: In a small saucepan, bring the cream just to a boil over medium heat. In a small bowl, whisk together the cornstarch and water, and add to the cream, whisking constantly. Return the mixture to the boil, whisk, and simmer for a few seconds, taking care not to burn the mixture on the bottom of the pan. Remove from the heat. Stir in the bourbon and 3 tablespoons of the sugar. Taste to make sure the sauce is sweet enough. If not, add more sugar, a teaspoon at a time.

SERVE THE PUDDING with sauce. It will have a thin consistency and will be absorbed by the pudding.

6	CUPS DAY-OLD FRENCH BREAD TORN INTO SMALL CHUNKS (ONE 10- TO 12-OUNCE LOAF)
4	LARGE EGGS
3	CUPS MILK
1/2	CUP (1 STICK) UNSALTED BUTTER, MELTED
1 1/2	CUPS SUGAR
1 1/2	TABLESPOONS VANILLA EXTRACT
2	TABLESPOONS GROUND CINNAMON
1/2	TEASPOON GROUND GINGER
2	TEASPOONS FRESHLY GRATED NUTMEG

⁎ tuffy's bourbon sauce

1	CUP HEAVY CREAM
1 1/2	TEASPOONS CORNSTARCH
1	TABLESPOON WATER
1/4	CUP BOURBON
3–4	TABLESPOONS SUGAR

chilled chocolate bread pudding by mom

ONE OF MY EARLIEST culinary memories is of my mother's cold chocolate bread pudding, dark and creamy, garnished with a fluffy dollop of sweetened whipped cream. It was a Sunday dinner dessert, and whether it was prompted by leftover bread or the fact that it could be made ahead on Saturday, it was delicious. It must have been adapted from *The Fannie Farmer Cookbook*, since my mother relied on the recipes of that venerable teacher and author. Here is my version of a family favorite.

———*

PLACE THE OVEN RACK in the middle position and preheat the oven to 350°F. Butter or spray the ramekins.

POUR 1½ CUPS of the milk into a large bowl. Add the bread, chocolate, and granulated sugar. Pour the mixture into a double boiler insert over simmering water. Cook, stirring, until the chocolate is melted and the mixture is well blended and smooth, about 5 minutes. Stir in the 2 tablespoons butter. Remove the insert from the water and set aside, but maintain the water at a simmer.

IN A SMALL BOWL, whisk the eggs until slightly thickened. Whisk in the salt, vanilla, and the remaining ¼ cup of milk. Whisk in ¼ cup of the chocolate mixture. Then, very slowly, stir this egg mixture into the chocolate mixture.

REPLACE THE INSERT over the simmering water and cook the pudding until slightly thick, about 10 minutes.

ingredients

2	TABLESPOONS UNSALTED BUTTER, SOFTENED, PLUS EXTRA SOFTENED BUTTER OR VEGETABLE-OIL COOKING SPRAY FOR THE RAMEKINS
1¾	CUPS WHOLE MILK
2	CUPS DAY-OLD TORN WHITE BREAD, (ABOUT 4 SLICES, CRUSTS REMOVED)
3	1-OUNCE SQUARES UNSWEETENED CHOCOLATE, CHOPPED
1	CUP GRANULATED SUGAR
3	LARGE EGGS
1/4	TEASPOON SALT
1	TEASPOON VANILLA EXTRACT
1	CUP HEAVY CREAM
1/4	TEASPOON GROUND CINNAMON
1	TABLESPOON CONFECTIONERS' SUGAR
6	4-OUNCE RAMEKINS

SET THE PREPARED RAMEKINS in a large baking pan lined with a dish towel. Ladle the chocolate mixture into the ramekins. Place the pan on the oven rack. Carefully add enough hot water to come halfway up the sides of the ramekins.

BAKE THE PUDDINGS UNTIL SET, and a knife inserted near the edge comes out clean, about 20 minutes. Using a dish towel, carefully remove the ramekins from the water bath and cool on a baking rack until room temperature. Cover the puddings with plastic wrap and refrigerate for up to 24 hours.

WHEN YOU ARE almost ready to serve, whip the cream with an electric mixer or a whisk until it holds soft peaks. Beat in the cinnamon and confectioners' sugar.

SERVE THE PUDDINGS chilled with the whipped cream.

YOU MAY ALSO bake the pudding in a 1½-quart glass dish for the same length of time.

SERVE IT WARM, if you prefer.

ingredients

VEGETABLE-OIL COOKING SPRAY FOR THE BAKING DISH

6 DAY-OLD CROISSANTS

8 OUNCES HIGH-QUALITY SEMISWEET CHOCOLATE CHIPS OR BITTERSWEET CHOCOLATE BARS, CHOPPED

2 TABLESPOONS UNSALTED BUTTER

8 LARGE EGGS

3 CUPS HEAVY CREAM

3/4 CUP SUGAR

1/4 CUP CHOCOLATE LIQUEUR, SUCH AS GODIVA

COLD WHIPPED CREAM FOR GARNISH (OPTIONAL)

*serves 8

chocolate croissant bread pudding

CROISSANTS LEND A TOUCH of elegance to this rich concoction, inspired by Chef Joachim Splichal's elegant preparation served at Patina Restaurant in Los Angeles. This decadently delicious adaptation would be a perfect ending to a Valentine's dinner.

———————●————

PLACE THE OVEN RACK in the middle position and preheat the oven to 350°F. Lightly spray a 9-x-13-inch baking dish with cooking spray.

SLICE THE CROISSANTS in half lengthwise. Place them on a baking sheet and toast them until golden, about 8 minutes. Remove from the oven and place them in the baking dish, breaking some up to fill in holes.

IN THE DOUBLE BOILER insert, over simmering water, melt the chocolate and butter.

IN A LARGE BOWL, whisk together the eggs, cream, sugar, and liqueur until smooth. Slowly whisk ¼ cup of the chocolate mixture into the egg mixture to temper it. Slowly stir the tempered egg mixture into the chocolate mixture and continue stirring until smooth. Pour the chocolate-egg mixture slowly over the croissants. Using the back of a spoon, submerge the croissants in the liquid for maximum absorption.

PLACE THE BAKING DISH in a larger shallow pan such as a roasting pan, and place it on the oven rack. Pour enough hot water into the larger pan to reach halfway up the sides of the baking dish. Bake the pudding for 45 minutes to 1 hour, or just until the center is set when gently shaken. Remove the baking dish from the water bath and serve the pudding immediately, or let cool on a baking rack until room temperature. Serve with the whipped cream, if desired.

SOFTENED BUTTER OR VEGETABLE-
OIL SPRAY FOR THE BAKING DISH

6 CUPS TORN-UP PIECES OF DAY-OLD
HIGH-QUALITY RAISIN BREAD
(ABOUT 12 SLICES, CRUSTS REMOVED)

3½ CUPS HIGH-QUALITY
PURCHASED EGGNOG

3 LARGE EGGS

2 LARGE EGG YOLKS

1/2 CUP SUGAR

3 TABLESPOONS BRANDY

3 TABLESPOONS DARK RUM

1 TEASPOON FRESHLY GRATED NUTMEG

FRESHLY WHIPPED CREAM,
OR TUFFY'S BOURBON SAUCE
(PAGE 42) FOR SERVING

*serves 10-12

raisin-eggnog bread pudding

HERE'S THE PERFECT festive dessert for a holiday buffet. It can be assembled early, and then put in the oven while guests are gathering. If you prefer, serve the pudding at room temperature, or even cold. Since this makes enough for 10 to 12, it's the ideal dish to bring along to a potluck supper.

BUTTER OR SPRAY a 13-x-9-x-2-inch baking dish.

PUT THE BREAD in a large bowl. Pour the eggnog over the bread and allow to soak for about 1 hour, or until all the liquid is absorbed.

PLACE THE OVEN RACK in the middle position and preheat the oven to 350°F.

IN A LARGE BOWL, whisk together the eggs, yolks, sugar, brandy, and rum until thick and smooth. Stir in the bread mixture and pour into the prepared dish. Sprinkle the top with the nutmeg. Place the dish in a large shallow pan, such as a roasting pan, lined with a dish towel. Place the pan on the oven rack, and pour enough hot water into the larger pan to come halfway up the sides of the pudding dish.

BAKE THE PUDDING for 1 hour, or just until the center is set when gently shaken. Transfer to a baking rack to cool slightly. Serve with a bowl of freshly whipped cream or Tuffy's Bourbon Sauce.

chapter 4: the sweet side

the crunch on crème brûlée

THERE ARE SEVERAL WAYS to obtain the crunchy caramel topping on crème brûlée. Try different methods and use the one that suits you best. You can also experiment with different types of sugars (see below). Be aware that the crèmes can be made up to 24 hours ahead and refrigerated, and then "brûléed" at the last minute. Indeed, if you brown them much more than an hour ahead, the sugar tends to melt and "weep." If the crèmes have been covered with plastic wrap or aluminum foil, be sure and blot any condensation on their surface with paper towels before applying the sugar.

the torch

With a little practice, you can master the small butane torch sold at kitchenware stores. Sprinkle the sugar over the chilled custard, then, holding the torch about 3 to 4 inches from the custard's surface, spray the flame back and forth over the sugar until you see a brown, bubbly crust. This can take anywhere from 2 to 4 minutes, depending on the heat of the torch. You can also use a larger propane torch you may have in the garage or workshop, but again, this takes practice. In his cookbook *How to Cook Everything* (1987) Mark Bittman suggests making the custard in one large bowl the first few times, until you have mastered the torch technique. When working with ramekins or custard cups, it's a matter of keeping a steady, even spray.

the broiler

This is probably the most convenient method for most cooks. After sprinkling the sugar on the chilled custards (make sure they are completely covered with it), set them on a baking sheet. Bittman suggests setting the pan under a cold broiler. He believes this technique does not cook the custard further, as a red-hot broiler would do. Put the oven rack in the next to the highest position, set the baking sheet on top, and turn on the broiler. Broil the crèmes, watching constantly and rotating the pan for even caramelization, until the tops are brittle and a rich brown, about 3 to 4 minutes, depending on the heat of the broiler.

making the tops ahead

Some people feel more confident following this method, even if it is a bit more work: Cover a baking sheet with foil and trace the shapes of the bottoms of the ramekins or custard cups you will be using. Smear softened butter over the traced areas, and then sprinkle with sugar. Place the pan under a preheated broiler, and broil until the rounds of sugar are bubbly and a rich brown color, about 2 to 3 minutes, depending on the heat of the broiler. Remove the pan and cool completely, until the rounds are hardened. You may then transfer them to a plate with a spatula, and just before serving, slide them onto the crèmes.

choosing the right sugar

Brown or white? The jury is still out on whether brown sugar (light or dark) or white gives you a better caramelized topping for crème brûlée. Follow the recommendation in each recipe, or feel free to experiment.

SUPERFINE: Some recipes call for superfine sugar. You can purchase it in the baking section of your supermarket, or make your own by simply processing regular granulated white sugar in the food processor for 10 seconds.

TURBINADO: Many crème brûlée aficionados prefer this partially refined, steam-cleaned type of light brown sugar. It has larger crystals that melt and caramelize easily and a delicate molasses flavor. Turbinado is readily available in the supermarket.

drying brown sugar

Since brown sugar has more moisture than white granulated sugar, and moisture impedes caramelization, here is a technique worth knowing if you choose brown sugar for the topping: Preheat the oven to about 350°F and turn it off. Spread out the brown sugar in a small baking pan and put it in the oven until the sugar dries, about 20 minutes. Remove from the oven and cool for about 6 to 8 minutes. Transfer the sugar to a resealable plastic bag. Seal the bag and crush the sugar until fine with a rolling pin. Store the sugar in an airtight container until you are ready to top the custards.

torch tips

If you are using a handheld butane torch to caramelize your crème brûlée, here are a few helpful tips:

- Caramelize your crèmes no more than an hour or two before serving; if caramelized too far in advance, the sugar may "weep."

- Make sure there are no flammable objects within the flame's reach.

- To protect your countertop, place the ramekins on a metal baking sheet before you caramelize the sugar.

- Hold the flame close to the surface of the crème, about 3 to 4 inches away, and move it in small circles over the surface until the sugar has melted evenly. It will bead together and form a rich, dark golden crust. The sugar will harden in a few seconds and the crème will be ready to serve.

- Take extra caution when using the torch with recipes containing alcohol; if held too close, the flame may cause the sugar to spatter.

Now that you have the torch, here are a few more things you can do with it, which may prove useful:

- The torch will melt and brown cheese on top of onion soup, casseroles, and gratin dishes.

- The torch will brown a meringue-topped dessert or glaze a fruit tart.

- To easily remove the skins of bell peppers, blacken them first with the torch, and then place them in a plastic bag for 10 minutes before peeling.

- The torch will crisp the skin of any roast.

*serves 6

grand marnier crème brûlée

WHEN THE SMALL crème brûlée torches first appeared in gourmet cookware shops, they were an instant success. Many of my cooking class students had received the torches as Christmas gifts one year, but no one was quite sure how to use them. We agreed to have a crème brûlée class where the focus would be on learning how to use the torch to achieve a perfect caramel crust on the classic dessert. Anyone looking in my kitchen window that frosty evening might have mistaken us for a coven of witches as the torches blazed away. Everyone left, torch in hand, feeling much more confident. Here is the recipe we used.

PLACE THE OVEN RACK in the middle position and preheat the oven to 325°F. Lightly butter or spray the ramekins.

IN A MEDIUM SAUCEPAN heat the cream over medium heat just until steam begins to rise. Remove the cream from the heat, add the orange zest, and allow to steep, covered, for 10 minutes.

IN A MEDIUM BOWL, whisk the egg yolks until slightly thickened. Add the superfine sugar and continue whisking until dissolved. Slowly whisk in the warm cream and the Grand Marnier.

SET THE PREPARED ramekins in a baking pan lined with a dish towel. Ladle the cream mixture into the ramekins. Place the pan on the oven rack and carefully pour enough hot water into the pan to come halfway up the sides of the ramekins. Bake, uncovered, until the crèmes are just barely set, about 30 to 35 minutes.

ingredients

	SOFTENED BUTTER OR VEGETABLE-OIL COOKING SPRAY FOR THE RAMEKINS
3	CUPS HEAVY CREAM
1 1/2	TABLESPOONS FINELY GRATED ORANGE ZEST
6	LARGE EGG YOLKS
6	TABLESPOONS SUPERFINE SUGAR (SEE PAGE 51)
2	TABLESPOONS GRAND MARNIER OR COINTREAU LIQUEUR
1/4	CUP LIGHT BROWN SUGAR, DRIED (SEE PAGE 51)
6	4-OUNCE RAMEKINS

CAREFULLY REMOVE the baking pan from the oven. Using a dish towel, carefully remove the ramekins from the hot water and cool to room temperature on a baking rack. Cover the ramekins with plastic wrap and refrigerate until chilled, about 2 hours, or even overnight.

WHEN READY TO SERVE, place the oven rack in the second-highest position and preheat the broiler. Remove the chilled crèmes from the refrigerator, uncover, and gently blot any moisture on the surface with a paper towel. Spread each crème evenly with 2 teaspoons of the dried brown sugar. Set the ramekins on a baking sheet and slide it under the broiler. Broil, watching constantly and rotating the pan for even caramelization, until the toppings are bubbling and a rich brown, about 2 to 3 minutes, depending on the intensity of the heat.

ALTERNATIVELY, brown the tops with a torch for about 1 to 2 minutes. If you choose to use a torch, be extremely careful as the sugar may spatter because of the alcohol in the crème mixture.

SERVE the crèmes immediately, or hold for up to 1 hour.

lemongrass and ginger crème brûlée

MY CHILDREN ARE very innovative cooks. My son, CH, and his wife Lisa, offered this recipe, which sounded intriguing to me. They reported that in the testing process, however, they'd had a bit of a problem. My seven-year-old grandson, Jake, trying to be helpful, had inadvertently dumped the infused lemongrass and ginger into the egg mixture. People were picking bits of lemongrass out of their teeth all evening! The second taste test was the charm. Lisa suggests putting a slice of the steeped ginger in the bottom of each ramekin, but be sure to tell your guests it is there. The Asian flavor, unusual in a custard, titillates the tongue in this lovely dish. Thanks, kids!

PLACE THE OVEN RACK in the middle position and preheat the oven to 325°F. Lightly butter or spray the ramekins.

PUT THE LEMONGRASS in a mortar or shallow dish and crush the slices with a pestle or the back of a large spoon to release the oils.

IN A MEDIUM SAUCEPAN, combine the bruised lemongrass, ginger, vanilla, and cream. Heat over medium heat just until steam begins to rise. Remove from the heat and let the mixture steep for 20 minutes.

IN A MEDIUM BOWL, whisk the egg yolks until slightly thickened. Whisk in the superfine sugar and continue whisking until dissolved.

{continued}

	SOFTENED BUTTER OR VEGETABLE-OIL COOKING SPRAY FOR THE RAMEKINS
1	CUP THINLY SLICED LEMONGRASS (WHITE AND GREEN PARTS)
1	3-INCH PIECE FRESH GINGER, PEELED AND SLICED
1/2	TEASPOON VANILLA EXTRACT
1 1/2	CUPS HEAVY CREAM
6	LARGE EGG YOLKS
6	TABLESPOONS SUPERFINE SUGAR (SEE PAGE 51)
1/4	CUP TURBINADO SUGAR
	CANDIED GINGER FOR GARNISH (OPTIONAL)
6	4-OUNCE RAMEKINS

lemongrass and ginger crème brûlée {continued}

STRAIN THE CREAM MIXTURE into a large measuring cup or bowl, pressing the solids with the back of a spoon to release their flavor. If you wish, reserve the ginger for the ramekins.

SLOWLY WHISK the infused cream into the egg yolk mixture.

SET THE PREPARED RAMEKINS in a baking pan lined with a dish towel. Ladle the cream mixture into the ramekins. Place the pan on the oven rack and carefully pour enough hot water into the pan to come halfway up the sides of the ramekins. Bake, uncovered, until the centers are just barely set, about 30 to 35 minutes.

CAREFULLY REMOVE the baking pan from the oven. Using a dish towel, carefully remove the ramekins from the hot water and cool to room temperature on a baking rack. Cover the ramekins with plastic wrap and refrigerate until chilled, about 2 hours, or even overnight.

WHEN READY TO SERVE, place the oven rack in the second-highest position and preheat the broiler. Remove the chilled crèmes from the refrigerator, uncover, and gently blot any moisture on the surface with a paper towel. Sprinkle each one with 2 teaspoons of the turbinado sugar. Set the ramekins on a baking sheet and slide it under the broiler. Broil, watching constantly and rotating the pan for even caramelization, until the toppings are bubbling and a rich brown, about 2 or 3 minutes, depending on the intensity of the heat. Alternatively, brown the tops with a torch for about 1 to 2 minutes.

SERVE the crèmes immediately, garnished with candied ginger, if desired.

ingredients

SOFTENED BUTTER OR
VEGETABLE-OIL COOKING SPRAY
FOR THE RAMEKINS

2 1/2   CUPS HEAVY CREAM

1/2   CUP GRANULATED SUGAR

PINCH OF SALT

1/2   CUP ALMOND PASTE

8   LARGE EGG YOLKS

2   TABLESPOONS AMARETTO LIQUEUR

1/4   CUP PLUS 4 TEASPOONS
LIGHT BROWN SUGAR,
DRIED (SEE PAGE 51)

8   4-OUNCE RAMEKINS

amaretto crème brûlée

I THINK OF THIS DISH as a perfect ending to a special dinner. Amaretto fans are legion, and the popular liqueur is now widely available in this country; indeed, much of it is produced here. Although it has a deep almond flavor, it is often made with the kernels of apricot pits. If you do not want to purchase a full-size bottle of Amaretto, a convenient "nip" size, available at most liquor stores, will provide you with a little over 3½ tablespoons. The almond paste can be found in the baking section of the supermarket in cans or plastic tubes. You can freeze any that remains.

PLACE THE OVEN RACK in the middle position and preheat the oven to 325°F. Lightly butter or spray the ramekins.

IN A MEDIUM SAUCEPAN, combine the cream, granulated sugar, salt, and almond paste. Heat gently over low heat, stirring and mashing the almond paste against the side of the pan until it melts, about 8 minutes. Do not let the mixture boil. Alternatively, you may use a double boiler. Remove from heat.

IN A MEDIUM BOWL, beat together the egg yolks and Amaretto. Whisk ¼ of the warm cream mixture into the beaten egg mixture, then slowly whisk the egg mixture into the cream mixture.

SET THE PREPARED RAMEKINS in a baking pan lined with a dish towel. Ladle the cream mixture into the ramekins. Place the pan on the oven rack and carefully pour enough hot water into the pan to come halfway up the sides of the ramekins. Bake, uncovered, until the crèmes are just barely set, about 30 to 35 minutes.

{continued}

amaretto crème brûlée {continued}

REMOVE THE BAKING PAN from the oven. Using a dish towel, carefully remove the ramekins from the hot water and cool to room temperature on a baking rack. Cover the ramekins with plastic wrap and refrigerate until chilled, about 2 hours, or even overnight.

WHEN READY TO SERVE, place the oven rack in the second-highest position and preheat the broiler. Remove the chilled crèmes from the refrigerator, uncover, and gently blot any moisture on the surface with a paper towel. Sprinkle each one evenly with 2 teaspoons of the dried brown sugar. Set the ramekins on a baking sheet and slide it under the broiler. Broil, watching constantly and rotating the pan for even caramelization, until the tops are bubbling and a rich brown, about 2 or 3 minutes, depending on the intensity of the heat.

ALTERNATIVELY, if you choose to use a torch instead, be extremely careful as the sugar may spatter because of the alcohol in the crème mixture.

SERVE the crèmes immediately, or hold for up to 1 hour.

ingredients

✳ cranberry sauce

3/4	CUP SUGAR
1/4	CUP ORANGE JUICE CONCENTRATE
1	CUP COLD WATER
12	OUNCES FRESH CRANBERRIES

✳ custard

●	SOFTENED BUTTER OR VEGETABLE-OIL COOKING SPRAY FOR THE RAMEKINS
4	CUPS HEAVY CREAM
1/2	VANILLA BEAN
8	LARGE EGG YOLKS
1/2	CUP SUGAR, PLUS 8 TEASPOONS FOR CARAMELIZATION
8	4-OUNCE RAMEKINS

serves 8

chef june's cranberry crème brûlée

CHEF JUNE JACOBS, CCP, and I have known each other for years through the International Association of Cooking Professionals (IACP). My daughter took Chef June's cooking classes when both were living in the Boston area. June is the author of *Feastivals Cooks at Home* (2001), a delightful cookbook highlighting celebrations. This recipe won a "Best of State" award in Martini and Rossi's State of Dessert contest. It was later featured on the menu at Jasper White's wonderful restaurant Jasper's in Boston. If you decide to make it when fresh cranberries are not in season, frozen ones, available in many supermarkets, will be just fine. The recipe will make more cranberry sauce than you need. It is delicious as a topping for ice cream, custard, or in a turkey sandwich.

———✳———

TO MAKE THE CRANBERRY SAUCE: In a large nonreactive (stainless steel or enamel) saucepan, combine the sugar, orange juice concentrate, and water. Stir to dissolve the sugar and bring to a boil. Add the cranberries, and return the mixture to a boil.

REDUCE THE HEAT and simmer gently for about 12 minutes. It will thicken and become glossy.

REMOVE from the heat. Cool to room temperature and chill. You will have about 2¼ cups of cranberry sauce, and will need about 1½ cups for the custards.

{continued}

chef june's cranberry crème brûlée {continued}

TO MAKE THE CUSTARD: Place the oven rack in the middle position and preheat the oven to 350°F. Lightly butter or spray the ramekins.

POUR THE CREAM into a medium-size pan. Using a sharp knife, slit the vanilla bean in half lengthwise and scrape the tiny seeds into the pan; add the bean pod. Bring the mixture to a boil over high heat. Remove from the heat immediately and set aside for 15 minutes. Discard the bean pod.

WHILE THE VANILLA bean is steeping in the cream, in a large bowl, combine the egg yolks and ½ cup sugar and whisk until blended. Slowly add the cream and vanilla mixture and mix well.

SET THE RAMEKINS in a baking pan lined with a dish towel. Ladle the custard into the ramekins. Place the pan on the oven rack and carefully add enough hot water to come halfway up the sides of the ramekins. Bake, uncovered, for 30 minutes, or until the crèmes are set, but not brown.

CAREFULLY REMOVE the baking pan from the oven. Using a dish towel, carefully remove the ramekins from the hot water and cool to room temperature on a baking rack. Cover the ramekins with plastic wrap and refrigerate until chilled for at least 2 hours, or even overnight.

BEFORE SERVING, preheat the broiler. Set the oven rack within 1 to 1½ inches from the heat. Remove the crèmes from the refrigerator, uncover, and gently blot any moisture on the surface with a paper towel. Spread about 2 tablespoons of the cranberry sauce evenly on each custard. Sprinkle the top of each ramekin with 1 teaspoon of sugar. Place the ramekins on a baking sheet and slide it under the broiler. Broil, watching constantly and rotating the pan for even caramelization, until the toppings are bubbling and a rich brown, about 2 minutes. Alternatively, brown the tops with a torch for about 1 to 2 minutes.

SERVE IMMEDIATELY or hold for up to 1 hour.

ingredients

SOFTENED BUTTER OR
VEGETABLE-OIL COOKING SPRAY
FOR THE RAMEKINS

2 CUPS HEAVY CREAM

6 LARGE EGG YOLKS

1/4 CUP SUPERFINE SUGAR

1/2 CUP MANGO PUREE (SEE NOTE)

1/4 CUP DARK BROWN SUGAR,
DRIED (SEE PAGE 51)

6 4-OUNCE RAMEKINS

NOTE: Mango puree is available frozen and in aseptic packaging in Latin markets and some specialty stores, but you can easily make your own: One ripe mango yields approximately ½ cup of pulp. To peel a ripe mango, stand it upright on a cutting surface. Cut vertical slices all around the pit to remove the flesh. Scrape the flesh off of the skin. Chop the pulp and put it in a blender or food processor. Add 1½ tablespoons of sugar and 1 tablespoon of fresh lemon juice. Process for 30 seconds, or until smooth. Makes about ½ cup of pulp.

*serves 6

mango crème brûlée

IN THIS RECIPE, the lush, tropical flavor of mango combines with the silky smoothness of a classic crème brûlée. The mango puree lies at the bottom of the dish, creating a refreshing surprise. There are several types of mangos readily available at the supermarket, any one of which will work here. They are ripe when they yield gently to finger pressure.

PLACE THE OVEN RACK in the middle position and preheat the oven to 325°F. Lightly butter or spray the ramekins.

IN A SMALL SAUCEPAN, heat the cream just until steam begins to rise.

IN A MEDIUM BOWL, whisk the egg yolks until slightly thickened. Whisk in the superfine sugar. Slowly whisk the cream into the beaten egg yolks.

SET THE RAMEKINS in a large baking pan lined with a dish towel. Spread 1 tablespoon of mango puree on the bottom of each ramekin. Ladle the cream mixture over the mango puree. Place the pan on the oven rack and carefully pour enough hot water into the pan to come halfway up the sides of the ramekins.

BAKE, uncovered, until the crèmes are just barely set, about 30 to 35 minutes. Carefully remove the pan from the oven. Using a dish towel, carefully remove the ramekins from the hot water and cool to room temperature on a baking rack. Cover the ramekins with plastic wrap and refrigerate until chilled, about 2 hours, or even overnight.

{continued}

mango crème brûlée {continued}

WHEN READY TO SERVE, place the oven rack in the second-highest position and preheat the broiler. Remove the chilled crèmes from the refrigerator, uncover, and gently blot any moisture on the surface of the crèmes with a paper towel.

SPRINKLE each one evenly with 2 teaspoons of the dried brown sugar. Set the ramekins on a baking sheet and slide it under the broiler. Broil, watching constantly and rotating the pan for even caramelization, until the toppings are bubbling and a rich brown, about 2 to 3 minutes, depending on the intensity of the heat. Alternatively, brown the tops with a torch for about 1 to 2 minutes. Serve the crèmes immediately, or hold for up to 1 hour.

corner house white chocolate–raspberry chambord crème brûlée

IF I WERE TO conjure up the quintessential New England inn, the Corner House in Center Sandwich, New Hampshire, would be it. Jane and Don Brown, the gracious hosts, offer a delicious menu year-round. Whether you dine in one of several attractive dining rooms, or upstairs in the cozy pub, the atmosphere is delightful. My assistant, Liz Lapham, and I were celebrating her birthday one day in July when Don presented us with this extraordinary dessert. He graciously agreed to share the recipe with me.

PLACE THE OVEN RACK in the middle position and preheat the oven to 325°F. Lightly butter or spray the ramekins.

IN A MEDIUM SAUCEPAN over low heat or in the top of a double boiler, heat the cream, ½ cup of the sugar, the honey, and chocolate until hot and steam rises, stirring occasionally, about 5 minutes. Do not boil.

IN A LARGE BOWL, whisk the egg yolks until slightly thickened. Slowly add the warm cream mixture, whisking constantly.

SET THE RAMEKINS in a large baking pan lined with a dish towel. Place several berries and a dash of the Chambord into each ramekin. Ladle the cream mixture into the ramekins. Place the pan on the oven rack and carefully pour enough hot water into the pan to come halfway up the sides of the ramekins.

BAKE, uncovered, for 35 minutes.

{continued}

ingredients

SOFTENED BUTTER OR VEGETABLE-OIL COOKING SPRAY FOR THE RAMEKINS

2½ CUPS HEAVY CREAM

3/4 CUP SUGAR

1/4 CUP HONEY

2 OUNCES WHITE CHOCOLATE, CHOPPED

5 LARGE EGG YOLKS

1 PINT FRESH RASPBERRIES OR WHOLE FROZEN BERRIES, THAWED

2 TABLESPOONS CHAMBORD LIQUEUR

optional garnishes

WHIPPED CREAM

FRESH RASPBERRIES

MINT LEAVES

6 4-OUNCE RAMEKINS

corner house white chocolate–raspberry chambord crème brûlée {continued}

CAREFULLY REMOVE the baking pan from the oven. The custards may appear a little loose, but they will firm up after chilling. Using a dish towel, carefully remove the ramekins from the water bath and cool to room temperature on a baking rack. Cover the ramekins with plastic wrap and refrigerate until chilled for at least 2 hours, or even overnight.

WHEN READY TO SERVE, place the oven rack in the second-highest position and preheat the broiler. Remove the chilled crèmes from the refrigerator, uncover, and gently blot any moisture on the surface with a paper towel. Sprinkle each one evenly with 2 teaspoons of the remaining sugar. Set the ramekins on a baking sheet and slide it under the broiler.

BROIL, watching constantly and rotating the pan for even caramelization, until the toppings are bubbling and a rich brown, about 2 or 3 minutes, depending on the intensity of the heat. Alternatively, brown the tops with a torch for about 1 to 2 minutes. Serve immediately, or hold for up to 1 hour.

GARNISH EACH RAMEKIN with whipped cream, a few fresh raspberries, and a sprig of mint, if desired.

ingredients

	SOFTENED BUTTER OR VEGETABLE-OIL COOKING SPRAY FOR THE RAMEKINS
6	LARGE EGG YOLKS
1	LARGE EGG
2/3	CUP GRANULATED SUGAR
1 3/4	CUPS HEAVY CREAM
1 3/4	CUPS MILK
1 1/2	TABLESPOONS INSTANT ESPRESSO POWDER
2	TABLESPOONS KAHLUA
1/4	CUP PLUS 4 TEASPOONS FIRMLY PACKED DARK BROWN SUGAR, DRIED (SEE PAGE 51)
8	4-OUNCE RAMEKINS

marie's cappuccino crème brûlée

MARIE GERLI, a neighbor of mine in our small New Hampshire town, is an extraordinary caterer. Her food is unusual, beautifully presented, and above all, delicious! For occasions ranging from a small engagement party for my daughter to a wedding for hundreds on Squam Lake (of *On Golden Pond* fame), Marie is much sought after to work her magic. This is one of her most popular creations.

PLACE THE OVEN RACK in the middle position and preheat the oven to 325°F. Lightly butter or spray the ramekins.

IN A MEDIUM BOWL, whisk together the yolks, whole egg, and sugar.

IN A HEAVY SAUCEPAN, heat the cream and milk together over moderately high heat just until the mixture comes to a boil. Stir in the espresso powder and Kahlua, and continue stirring until the powder is dissolved. Slowly add the milk mixture to the egg mixture in a steady stream, whisking constantly and skimming off any froth.

PLACE THE RAMEKINS in a baking pan lined with a dish towel. Ladle the crème mixture into the ramekins. Place the pan on the oven rack and carefully pour enough hot water into the pan to come halfway up the sides of the ramekins.

BAKE THE CRÈMES until just barely set, about 40 minutes.

{continued}

marie's cappuccino crème brûlée {continued}

CAREFULLY REMOVE the baking pan from the oven. With a dish towel, remove the ramekins from the hot water and cool to room temperature on a baking rack.

REFRIGERATE THE CRÈMES, covered loosely with plastic wrap, for at least 4 hours, or even overnight.

WHEN READY TO SERVE, place the oven rack in the second-highest position and preheat the broiler. Remove the chilled crèmes from the refrigerator, uncover, and gently blot any moisture on the surface with a paper towel. Sprinkle each one evenly with 2 teaspoons of the dried brown sugar. Set the ramekins on a baking sheet and slide it under the broiler. Broil, watching constantly and rotating the pan for even caramelization, until the toppings are bubbling and a rich brown, about 2 or 3 minutes, depending on the intensity of the heat.

ALTERNATIVELY, brown the tops with a torch for about 1 to 2 minutes.

SERVE the crèmes immediately or hold for up to 30 minutes.

ingredients

SOFTENED BUTTER OR
VEGETABLE-OIL COOKING SPRAY
FOR THE RAMEKINS

6 TABLESPOONS CHOCOLATE MALT MIX

1 1/2 CUPS HEAVY CREAM

6 LARGE EGG YOLKS

1 TABLESPOON SUPERFINE SUGAR
(SEE PAGE 51)

1 TEASPOON VANILLA EXTRACT

1/4 CUP DARK BROWN SUGAR, DRIED
(SEE PAGE 51)

6 4-OUNCE RAMEKINS

ch's chocolate malted crème brûlée

MY SON, CH, and his wife, Lisa, first came across this recipe while on a ski vacation in Colorado. The restaurant they ate in served a tasting menu topped off with a "Trio of Crème Brûlées." While the flavors of the other two crèmes have faded from memory, the one they remember well was this delightful concoction based on a chocolate malt mix. When I asked them for a contribution for this book, they said this had to be included. They believe it is pretty close to the original they tasted on that frosty Colorado night.

PUT THE OVEN RACK in the middle position and preheat the oven to 300°F. Lightly butter or spray the ramekins.

IN A FOOD PROCESSOR, process the chocolate malt mix until very fine, about 15 to 20 seconds.

IN A SMALL SAUCEPAN, heat the cream just until steam begins to rise. Remove the cream from the heat and mix in the processed chocolate malt mix. Allow it to steep, covered, for 10 minutes.

MEANWHILE, in a medium bowl, whisk the egg yolks until slightly thickened. Add the superfine sugar and whisk until dissolved. Slowly whisk in the cream mixture, and then the vanilla.

SET THE PREPARED RAMEKINS in a baking pan lined with a dish towel. Ladle the crème mixture into the ramekins. Set the baking pan on the oven rack and pour enough hot water into the pan to come halfway up the sides of ramekins. Bake, uncovered, until the crèmes are just barely set, about 30 to 35 minutes.

{continued}

ch's chocolate malted crème brûlée {continued}

CAREFULLY REMOVE the baking pan from the oven, leaving the ramekins in the hot water, and cool to room temperature. Remove the ramekins, cover with plastic wrap, and refrigerate until chilled for at least 2 hours, or even overnight.

WHEN READY TO SERVE, place the oven rack in the second-highest position and preheat the broiler. Remove the chilled ramekins from the refrigerator, uncover, and gently blot any moisture with a paper towel. Sprinkle each ramekin evenly with 2 teaspoons of the brown sugar. Set the ramekins on a baking sheet and slide it under the broiler. Broil, watching constantly and rotating the pan for even caramelization, until the toppings are bubbly and a rich brown, about 2 to 3 minutes, depending on the intensity of the heat. Alternatively, brown the tops with a torch for about 1 to 2 minutes.

LET THE CRÈMES COOL on a baking rack for 10 minutes and serve, or refrigerate for up to 30 minutes.

chapter 5: the sweet relations

chocolate pots de crème 101

THIS IS THE EASIEST DESSERT you will ever make. Pots de crème, or "pots of cream," are traditionally cooked in small cups that have lids. The lids are placed over the cups as the dessert chills. Any small cup will do here, because the crème is not cooked in the oven. This is a wonderful opportunity to dig out that set of demitasse cups buried in the back of your china closet. If you have concerns about using eggs that have not been truly cooked, buy pasteurized eggs, available at most supermarkets. Gild the lily and add a small dollop of whipped cream topped by a chocolate-covered coffee bean or a sprinkle of chocolate shavings to each serving.

IN A BLENDER, blend the eggs, chocolate, and vanilla until smooth, about 30 seconds. Slowly add the hot half-and-half and continue blending until well mixed.

POUR THE CUSTARD into demitasse or pots de crème cups. Cover with lids or plastic wrap.

CHILL THE CRÈMES for at least 2 hours, or even overnight, before serving. If you like, garnish each crème with chocolate shavings or a small dollop of whipped cream and top with a chocolate-covered coffee bean.

ingredients

2 LARGE EGGS

6 OUNCES SEMISWEET MINI-CHOCOLATE CHIPS OR SEMISWEET CHOCOLATE BARS, FINELY CHOPPED

1 TEASPOON VANILLA EXTRACT

1 CUP HALF-AND-HALF, SCALDED (SEE PAGE 12)

CHOCOLATE SHAVINGS FOR GARNISH (OPTIONAL; SEE NOTE)

WHIPPED CREAM FOR GARNISH (OPTIONAL)

6 CHOCOLATE-COVERED COFFEE BEANS FOR GARNISH (OPTIONAL)

8 TWO-OUNCE DEMITASSE CUPS

NOTE: To make chocolate shavings, scrape a vegetable peeler lengthwise down a chocolate bar.

canyon ranch in the berkshires lime pots de crème

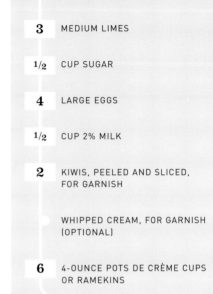

ingredients

SOFTENED BUTTER OR VEGETABLE-OIL COOKING SPRAY FOR THE CUPS

3 MEDIUM LIMES

1/2 CUP SUGAR

4 LARGE EGGS

1/2 CUP 2% MILK

2 KIWIS, PEELED AND SLICED, FOR GARNISH

WHIPPED CREAM, FOR GARNISH (OPTIONAL)

6 4-OUNCE POTS DE CRÈME CUPS OR RAMEKINS

FOR MORE THAN TWENTY YEARS, Canyon Ranch in the Berkshires Health Resort has been a celebrated leader in the healthy gourmet cuisine movement. This delightful spa cuisine dessert was created by pastry chef Laurie Erickson. You can have your pot de crème and eat it, too!

PLACE THE OVEN RACK in the middle position and preheat the oven to 275°F. Lightly butter or spray the cups.

USING A VEGETABLE PEELER, remove the zest from the limes, being careful not to cut into the white pith. Put the zest in a small saucepan of boiling water and boil for 5 minutes. While the zest is boiling, juice the limes. You should have about ⅔ cup of lime juice.

DRAIN THE ZEST in a sieve and blot dry. Blend the lime juice, zest, sugar, eggs, and milk in a blender for 5 minutes. Pour the mixture through a sieve into a bowl and ladle it into the pots de crème cups. Gently skim off any foam from the surface of the pots.

PLACE THE CUPS in a large baking pan lined with a dish towel. Place the pan on the oven rack and add enough hot water to come halfway up the sides of the cups.

BAKE THE POTS DE CRÈME, uncovered, for 30 minutes, or until a knife inserted close to the edge comes out clean. Remove the pan from the oven. Carefully remove the cups from the hot water with a dish towel and cool to room temperature on a baking rack.

SERVE IMMEDIATELY, or refrigerate, covered, for 2 to 4 hours and serve cold. Garnish each crème with a slice of kiwi and whipped cream, if desired.

ingredients

SOFTENED BUTTER OR
VEGETABLE-OIL COOKING SPRAY
FOR THE CUPS OR RAMEKINS

2 CUPS HEAVY CREAM

1/3 CUP PASSION FRUIT PUREE
(SEE NOTE)

5 LARGE EGG YOLKS

1/4 CUP PLUS 1 TABLESPOON SUGAR

6 4-OUNCE POTS DE CRÈME CUPS
OR RAMEKINS

NOTE: If you prefer to make your own passion
puree, it is a simple task. Fresh passion fruit is now
available in most supermarkets or Latino markets
from March through September. When purchasing,
choose large, plump, slightly wrinkled or "dimpled"
purple fruit and store in the refrigerator until
ready to use.

To puree, scoop the seeds and pulp from 3 or 4
ripe passion fruit into a sieve set over a bowl. With
the back of a wooden spoon push the pulp through
the sieve to separate the juice and pulp from the
seeds. You should have about 1/3 cup juicy pulp.

canoe's passion fruit pots de crème

WHEN CHEF SCOTT OUELLETTE recently opened Canoe in our small
town of Center Harbor, New Hampshire, on Lake Winnipesaukee, he
brought fresh ideas for wonderful food. He kindly agreed to share
this recipe with me. Frozen passion fruit puree is available at Latino
stores and some supermarkets.

PLACE THE OVEN RACK in the middle position and preheat the oven to 350°F.
Lightly butter or spray the cups or ramekins.

IN A MEDIUM SAUCEPAN, combine the heavy cream and passion fruit puree.
Heat the mixture just until steam begins to rise from the pan.

IN A MEDIUM BOWL, whisk the egg yolks until slightly thickened, and then whisk
in the sugar.

WHISK THE HOT CREAM mixture very slowly into the egg yolks. Return this mixture
to the pan and reheat until just barely simmering. Do not boil.

SET THE RAMEKINS or cups in a large baking pan lined with a dish towel. Ladle
the cream mixture into the cups. Place the pan on the oven rack and carefully
pour enough hot water into the pan to come halfway up the sides of the cups.
Bake, uncovered, for 30 minutes, or until a knife inserted close to the edge
comes out clean.

REMOVE THE BAKING PAN from the oven. Carefully remove the crèmes from
the hot water bath with a dish towel and cool to room temperature on a baking
rack. Cover the crèmes with plastic wrap and refrigerate until chilled, about
2 hours, or even overnight. Serve cold.

cranberry-mascarpone pots de crème

I AM TOTALLY ENAMORED of cranberries. I love the fresh tart flavor of this versatile fruit and use it in a multitude of ways. In addition to the obvious sauces, chutneys, and relishes, in my native New England the cranberries are used in muffins, pancakes, and breads. Dried cranberries, now found in supermarkets, are particularly adaptable to desserts, and their tart sweetness adds a delicious counterpoint to the rich creaminess of a custard-based dish. A pot de crème is traditionally served in a small cup with a lid, but any ramekin, custard cup, or ovenproof cup may be used. This festive pot de crème is a lovely addition to a holiday meal.

LIGHTLY BUTTER or spray the custard cups.

PUT THE CRANBERRIES in a shallow soup or cereal bowl, and pour the brandy or orange juice over them. Soak for 30 minutes, then drain and pat dry. Divide the cranberries among the prepared cups, arranging them on the bottom.

PUT THE OVEN RACK in the middle position and preheat the oven to 325°F. Whisk the eggs briefly in a large bowl. Add the mascarpone, yogurt, sugar, vanilla, and cinnamon and whisk until smooth.

PLACE THE CUPS in a large baking pan lined with a dish towel. Pour the mixture into the prepared cups, and sprinkle lightly with the grated nutmeg. Place the pan on the oven rack and carefully pour enough hot water into the pan to come halfway up the sides of the cups.

BAKE, uncovered, for 30 minutes, or until a knife inserted close to the edge comes out clean. Remove the cups from the pan with a dish towel. Cool completely and serve the crèmes at room temperature or refrigerate for up to 24 hours.

ingredients

	SOFTENED BUTTER OR VEGETABLE-OIL COOKING SPRAY FOR THE CUSTARD CUPS OR RAMEKINS
2/3	CUP DRIED CRANBERRIES
1/4	CUP BRANDY OR ORANGE JUICE, HEATED
3	LARGE EGGS
8	OUNCES MASCARPONE CHEESE
8	OUNCES VANILLA YOGURT
1/2	CUP SUGAR
1/2	TEASPOON VANILLA EXTRACT
1/4	TEASPOON GROUND CINNAMON
1/2	TEASPOON FRESHLY GRATED NUTMEG
8	POTS DE CRÈME CUPS OR SIX 4-OUNCE RAMEKINS

ingredients

- SOFTENED BUTTER OR VEGETABLE-OIL COOKING SPRAY FOR THE BAKING DISH
- **2** 15-OUNCE CANS PEAR HALVES IN LIGHT SYRUP
- **1/4** CUP ALL-PURPOSE FLOUR
- **1/4** CUP GRANULATED SUGAR
- **8** OUNCES MASCARPONE CHEESE
- **2** LARGE EGGS
- **1** TEASPOON VANILLA EXTRACT
- **1/2** TEASPOON GROUND CINNAMON
- **1/4** TEASPOON FRESHLY GRATED NUTMEG
- **3** TABLESPOONS LIGHT BROWN SUGAR

*serves 6-8

pear mascarpone custard

I ATTEND a gentle aerobics class several mornings a week at Karen Porrozo's studio in New Hampton, New Hampshire. Neither snow, nor sleet, nor rain keeps the group from attending, as much for the camaraderie and laughter as the exercise. Once a month we celebrate birthdays. Karen makes the coffee and we alternate bringing the goodies. The group has been supportive in testing my efforts for my cookbooks, even if we do have to exercise a little harder on those mornings. Here is a favorite dish I presented to the group, which could be served as a brunch accompaniment as well as a dessert.

———⚬———

PLACE THE OVEN RACK in the middle position and preheat the oven to 375°F. Lightly butter or spray an 11-x-7-x-1½-inch baking dish (2 quarts).

DRAIN THE PEAR HALVES, reserving ¾ cup of the syrup. Place the pear halves on a cutting surface, flat side down, and score the rounded sides with shallow, crosswise cuts. Arrange the pears in the prepared baking dish.

PUT THE FLOUR and the sugar in a blender or food processor and blend or process until combined. Add the mascarpone, eggs, vanilla, reserved pear syrup, cinnamon, and nutmeg. Blend or process until the batter is smooth, about 20 seconds. Do not overmix. Pour the batter over the fruit and sprinkle with the brown sugar.

BAKE THE CUSTARD until puffy and light brown and the center is set when gently shaken, about 25 to 30 minutes. Remove from the oven and cool on a baking rack for 5 to 10 minutes. Serve the custard warm.

1/2	CUP (1 STICK) UNSALTED BUTTER
3/4	CUP SUGAR
1 1/2	TEASPOONS JAPANESE *MATCHA*
2/3	CUP APRICOT NECTAR
2	TEASPOONS UNFLAVORED GELATIN
1/2	CUP HEAVY CREAM
1/2	CUP FRESH ORANGE JUICE
4	LARGE EGGS, LIGHTLY BEATEN
6	4-OUNCE RAMEKINS

*serves 6

cool and silken green tea custard

THE **VARIETY OF TEAS** and coffees at Mary Lou and Bob Heiss's Coffee Gallery in Northampton, Massachusetts, is amazing. Just cross the threshold of the store and you are enveloped by delicious aromas. Mary Lou created this velvety concoction to introduce her staff and customers to *Matcha*, a powdered Japanese green tea used in tea ceremonies. It is available at Asian markets and specialty stores, and can be ordered online at www.CooksShopHere.com (Mary Lou's store).

IN A DOUBLE BOILER insert over simmering water, melt the butter. Remove the insert from the water, and keep the water simmering over low heat.

IN A SMALL BOWL, mix the sugar and the *Matcha* until well blended and then add to the melted butter. Stir to blend well.

POUR THE APRICOT NECTAR into a small bowl, and sprinkle the gelatin over it to soften. Set aside.

ADD THE CREAM and orange juice to the melted butter mixture and then slowly add the beaten eggs. Replace the insert over the simmering water and cook, stirring constantly, until the mixture thickens and coats the back of a metal spoon, about 12 to 14 minutes.

STRAIN THE MIXTURE through a fine sieve into a bowl to ensure a silken texture. Add the apricot nectar and gelatin mixture to the cooked custard and stir well until the gelatin is dissolved and well incorporated into the custard. Set the cooked mixture aside and cool to room temperature.

POUR THE CUSTARD into the ramekins, cover with plastic wrap, and refrigerate for at least 2 hours, or even overnight. Serve cold.

SOFTENED BUTTER
FOR TWO BAKING DISHES

serves 4-6

italian prune plum custard

ITALIAN PLUMS, or prune plums, make a brief appearance during the early autumn days of September. Because the season is so short, I use them in cakes, tarts—any way I can think of. I feature this tart, juicy fruit in every class I teach in early fall. To pit the plums, run a sharp paring knife around the indentation of the plum, and then with both hands twist the plum halves in opposite directions. Remove the pit.

————⊛

PLACE THE OVEN RACK in the middle position and preheat the oven to 350°F. Lightly butter a medium baking dish.

TO MAKE THE FILLING: Arrange the pitted plum halves, skin side down, on the baking dish. Sprinkle with the cinnamon, sugar, lemon zest, and juice. Bake the plums for 15 minutes, or just until the fruit is tender but holds its shape. Lightly butter a 10- to 11-inch baking dish and transfer the fruit from the first baking dish; reserve the juices.

TO MAKE THE CUSTARD: Raise the oven temp to 375°F. In a medium bowl, whisk the eggs and the sugar to blend, then whisk in the flour, vanilla, and half-and-half. Continue whisking until well blended. Pour the mixture over the fruit. (You may cover the dish with plastic wrap and refrigerate at this point for up to 8 hours, if not baking immediately. Bring to room temperature before baking.) Bake the custard in the upper third of the oven for 20 to 25 minutes, or until it has puffed and browned slightly.

WHILE THE DESSERT is baking, in a small saucepan warm the reserved juices with liqueur if using.

SERVE THE CUSTARD warm or room temperature, accompanied by the warm juices and sweetened whipped cream, if desired.

⁂ filling

1	POUND PRUNE PLUMS, HALVED AND PITTED (SEE HEADNOTE)
1/8	TEASPOON GROUND CINNAMON
1/2	CUP SUGAR
	GRATED ZEST OF 1 LEMON
1	TABLESPOON FRESH LEMON JUICE

⁂ custard

2	LARGE EGGS
3	TABLESPOONS SUGAR
2	TABLESPOONS ALL-PURPOSE FLOUR
1	TEASPOON VANILLA EXTRACT
1/3	CUP HALF-AND-HALF
1/2	CUP COGNAC OR KIRSCH (OPTIONAL)
	WHIPPED CREAM FOR GARNISH (OPTIONAL)

ingredients

	VEGETABLE-OIL COOKING SPRAY FOR THE MOLD
3	CUPS MILK
1	VANILLA BEAN
1 1/2	CUPS SUGAR
2	TABLESPOONS WATER
1 1/2	TABLESPOONS LIGHT CORN SYRUP
1/4	TEASPOON FRESH LEMON JUICE
6	LARGE EGGS
	SEASONAL FRUITS, SUCH AS PEACHES, BLUEBERRIES, RASPBERRIES, AND MELON BALLS
	FRESH MINT LEAVES FOR GARNISH
4–6	CUP RING MOLD

*serves 8

weiss family crème caramel

PIERRE WIESS AND RICHARD RESSLER co-own Duck Soup, a delightful, cookware and gourmet foods emporium in Sudbury, Massachusetts. After World War II, Pierre and his family emigrated from the German section of Switzerland to France. Because of their German accent, the Weiss's new neighbors were less than welcoming. Fortunately, a local lady, "Mamie Mezelle," took them under her wing, and prepared this unforgettable classic dessert for Pierre when he was ill. His family has been making it ever since. The dessert is traditionally made in a ring mold, or you can use a 1½-quart soufflé dish.

LIGHTLY COAT the ring mold with the cooking spray.

IN A MEDIUM SAUCEPAN, bring the milk just to a boil and remove from the heat. Slit the vanilla bean in half over the pan of milk and scrape out the seeds with the tip of a knife to release them into the milk. Add the pod and steep the pod and seeds in the milk for 20 minutes.

MEANWHILE, in a small saucepan, combine ¾ cup of the sugar with the water, corn syrup, and lemon juice. Place the pan over medium heat and stir until the sugar is dissolved. Then stop stirring the mixture, and let it simmer. Leave undisturbed until it becomes a rich, amber brown, watching it carefully. Pour it into the prepared mold and rotate the mold to coat it evenly on the bottom and 1 inch up its sides. Place on a baking rack and let cool.

PLACE THE OVEN RACK in the middle position and preheat the oven to 325°F.

{continued}

weiss family crème caramel {continued}

IN A LARGE BOWL, whisk together the eggs until slightly thickened and then whisk in the remaining ¾ cup of sugar. Remove the vanilla bean pod and slowly pour the warm milk into the egg mixture in a stream, whisking constantly. Pour the custard through a fine sieve into another bowl, and then pour it into the prepared ring mold.

SET THE RING MOLD in a larger baking pan lined with a dish towel. Place the pan on the oven rack and pour in enough hot water to come halfway up the sides of the ring. Bake for 45 minutes, or until a knife inserted 1 inch from the edge comes out clean. Remove the pan from the oven. Carefully remove the ring mold from the water with oven mitts and let cool on a baking rack. Cover and chill for at least 3 hours, or even overnight.

JUST BEFORE SERVING, immerse the ring mold in hot water, shaking it slightly, for about 30 seconds, or until you can see the custard has loosened up. Run a thin knife around the inside of the mold and invert on a round platter. The caramel sauce will run down the sides of the custard. (There may be some hardened caramel that will adhere to the mold. Don't worry about this.) Fill the center with fresh fruits and garnish with mint leaves.

linda's splendid lo-carb custard

LINDA HUNTRESS, a member of our indomitable walking group, takes good care of her health, and that of her husband, Fred. They both enjoy something sweet at the end of a meal, and were loath to give it up when they embarked on a low-carb diet recently. While we were walking one day she quietly suggested that I might be interested in using a recipe she had devised using a low-carb artificial sweetener. I was skeptical at first but after tasting it, I'm ready to join the South Beach crowd! The use of Splenda instead of sugar cuts the carbs here, and produces a "splendid" guilt-free dessert.

PLACE THE OVEN RACK in the middle position and preheat the oven to 350°F. Lightly spray the ramekins with the vegetable oil.

IN A MEDIUM SAUCEPAN, heat the milk just until steam begins to rise. Remove from the heat and allow to cool.

WHISK THE EGGS in a medium bowl until slightly thickened. Add the Splenda, nutmeg, cinnamon, and vanilla, whisking until the Splenda is dissolved. Add the milk slowly to the egg mixture and whisk to blend.

SET THE PREPARED RAMEKINS in a baking pan lined with a dish towel. Ladle the custard mixture into the ramekins. Place the pan on the oven rack and carefully add enough hot water to come halfway up the sides of the ramekins. Bake, uncovered, until set and a knife inserted near the edge comes out clean, about 40 minutes.

REMOVE THE BAKING PAN from the oven. Using a dish towel, carefully remove the ramekins from the hot water and cool to room temperature on a baking rack. Cover the ramekins with plastic wrap and refrigerate until chilled, about 3 hours, or even overnight. To serve, garnish with toasted almonds, if desired.

ingredients

- BUTTER-FLAVORED SPRAY OR VEGETABLE-OIL COOKING SPRAY FOR THE RAMEKINS
- **2** CUPS SKIM OR 1% MILK
- **2** LARGE EGGS
- **6** PACKETS SPLENDA SWEETENER (SEE NOTE)
- **1/4** TEASPOON FRESHLY GRATED NUTMEG
- **1/2** TEASPOON GROUND CINNAMON
- **1** TEASPOON VANILLA EXTRACT
- **1/2** CUP SLICED ALMONDS, TOASTED, FOR GARNISH (OPTIONAL)
- **6** 4-OUNCE RAMEKINS

NOTE: If you have the loose packaged Splenda, use ¼ cup instead of the 6 packets. However the loose packaged product produces a slightly sweeter version than the packets.

ingredients

- SOFTENED BUTTER OR VEGETABLE-OIL COOKING SPRAY FOR THE RAMEKINS
- **2** CUPS HALF-AND-HALF
- **1/2** CUP PLUS 2 TABLESPOONS PURE MAPLE SYRUP
- **5** LARGE EGGS
- PINCH OF SALT
- **2** TABLESPOONS DARK RUM (OPTIONAL)
- WHIPPED CREAM FOR GARNISH (OPTIONAL)
- **6** WALNUT HALVES FOR GARNISH (OPTIONAL)
- **6** 4-OUNCE RAMEKINS

*serves 6

maple syrup custard

NEW ENGLANDERS LOVE their maple syrup, and do not restrict its use to waffles or pancakes. About mid-March, when the days are longer but the nights are still frosty, the sap starts to flow. Sugarhouses send up billows of smoke as the sap is boiled down over wood fires to produce the delicious syrup. "Sugaring off" is an annual event, and the amber-golden liquid is highly prized. In this delectable custard, maple syrup is used instead of sugar, so be sure to use pure maple syrup.

PLACE THE OVEN RACK in the middle position and preheat the oven to 325°F. Butter or spray the ramekins.

IN A MEDIUM SAUCEPAN over medium-low heat, warm the half-and-half and the ½ cup of maple syrup just until steam begins to rise.

IN A MEDIUM BOWL, whisk the eggs until slightly thickened. Add the salt and the rum, if desired. Slowly pour the hot syrup mixture into the eggs, whisking constantly.

SET THE RAMEKINS in a large baking pan lined with a dish towel. Set the pan on the oven rack and ladle the maple custard mixture into the ramekins. Carefully add enough hot water to come halfway up the sides of the ramekins. Bake for 25 to 30 minutes, until barely set. Carefully remove the pan from the oven and remove the ramekins from the water bath with a dish towel. Refrigerate immediately, covering the ramekins with plastic wrap after slightly cooled, at least 2 hours, or even overnight.

JUST BEFORE SERVING, garnish each custard with a dollop of whipped cream and walnut halves (if desired) and drizzle with a teaspoon of the remaining maple syrup.

george's diner grape-nut custard pudding

GEORGE'S DINER, near Lake Winnipesaukee in Meredith, New Hampshire, and Grape-Nut Pudding are both New England classics. There are as many recipes for this comforting dessert as there are people lined up to get into George's on any given day so they can have a bowl of this nostalgic pudding as well as other old-time favorites. Here is my interpretation of George's ultimate comfort food.

PLACE THE OVEN RACK in the middle position and preheat the oven to 350°F. Butter or spray a 1-quart baking dish.

PUT ½ CUP of the Grape-Nuts in a small bowl. In a small saucepan, scald the milk (see page 12) and pour it over the Grape-Nuts. Allow to cool.

MEANWHILE, in a medium bowl, whisk together the eggs, sugar, salt, vanilla, nutmeg, and cinnamon. Stir in the Grape-Nuts mixture and add the raisins, if using.

PLACE A LARGE BAKING PAN lined with a dish towel on the oven rack and place the prepared baking dish in it. Pour the pudding into the baking dish and sprinkle the top of the pudding with the remaining ½ cup of Grape-Nuts. Carefully add enough hot water to come halfway up the sides of the pudding dish. Bake for 40 to 45 minutes, or until the pudding is set. Serve warm or at room temperature, with whipped cream, if desired.

ingredients

SOFTENED BUTTER OR VEGETABLE-OIL COOKING SPRAY FOR THE BAKING DISH

1 CUP GRAPE-NUTS CEREAL

2 CUPS MILK

2 LARGE EGGS

1/3 CUP SUGAR

1/2 TEASPOON SALT

1 TEASPOON VANILLA EXTRACT

1/4 TEASPOON GROUND NUTMEG

1/2 TEASPOON GROUND CINNAMON

1/2 CUP RAISINS (OPTIONAL)

WHIPPED CREAM FOR GARNISH (OPTIONAL)

ingredients

2	CUPS MILK
3	LARGE EGGS, SEPARATED
1/2	CUP GRANULATED SUGAR
1	TABLESPOON CORNSTARCH
1	TABLESPOON WATER
	PINCH OF SALT
1	TEASPOON VANILLA EXTRACT
1	TEASPOON ORANGE EXTRACT
1/2	CUP CONFECTIONERS' SUGAR, SIFTED
1	1-OUNCE SQUARE UNSWEETENED CHOCOLATE, MELTED (SEE NOTE)

NOTE: Chocolate can be easily melted in the microwave. Put the chocolate in a glass dish. Microwave on high power for 1 to 2 minutes, stirring once.

whitworth family kiss pudding

THIS WHIMSICAL DESSERT is as elegant and fun as the person who gave me the recipe. Laura Whitworth is everything I want to be when I grow up. Now in her eighties, Laura is a lively addition to any event. She told me this was her family's favorite dessert over the years, and when you have presented it to your family and guests, you'll see why!

IN A DOUBLE BOILER insert over simmering water, heat the milk just until bubbles rise around the edge of the pan. In a small bowl, whisk the egg yolks lightly and whisk in the sugar.

IN A SMALL DISH, dissolve the cornstarch in the water. Whisk the cornstarch mixture and the salt into the egg yolks. Whisk 2 tablespoons of the hot milk into the egg mixture, and then slowly beat the egg mixture into the milk.

COOK THE CUSTARD, stirring gently but constantly, until thick enough to coat the back of a spoon, about 8 to 10 minutes. Remove from the heat. Stir in the vanilla and orange flavorings. Pour the custard into a bowl and cover with plastic wrap. Refrigerate until chilled, about 2 hours, or even overnight.

WHEN READY TO SERVE, using an electric mixer, beat the egg whites until stiff. With a rubber spatula, fold in the confectioners' sugar and then the melted chocolate, just until the "kiss" mixture is a light chocolate color.

PILE THE CHILLED CUSTARD into sherbet or wine glasses, and top with the egg white and chocolate "kiss" mixture. Serve immediately.

chapter 6: grand finales

ingredients

* ### islands

2	CUPS MILK
1	VANILLA BEAN
3	LARGE EGG WHITES
2/3	CUP SUGAR

* ### custard

	MILK (RESERVED FROM MAKING THE "ISLANDS" PLUS MORE AS NECESSARY)
1	VANILLA BEAN
5	LARGE EGG YOLKS
1/2	CUP SUGAR
	ICE CUBES FOR CHILLING CUSTARD
	FRESH STRAWBERRIES OR RASPBERRIES FOR SERVING (OPTIONAL)

*serves 6

laskin floating islands

MY SON-IN-LAW, Bill Laskin, contributed this recipe of his grandmother's. No Laskin family gathering was complete without her floating islands. She would arrive with two large recycled mayonnaise jars, one containing the custard, the other the meringue (Bill's grandmother didn't believe in Tupperware). Then it was just a matter of combining the contents to create the family's favorite dessert.

Fresh strawberries or raspberries are a delicious accompaniment. Bill advises that the custard will keep, refrigerated, for several days. However, the meringues tend to flatten out as they sit, so they are best served within a few hours of cooking.

TO MAKE THE ISLANDS: In an 8- or 9-inch skillet, heat the milk and vanilla bean over low heat until bubbles appear around the edge of the pan.

MEANWHILE, with an electric mixer, beat the egg whites in a medium bowl until foamy.

ADD THE SUGAR in a steady stream, beating until the egg whites are stiff.

REMOVE THE SKILLET from the heat, and use a large serving spoon to drop half the beaten egg whites onto the milk in 3 large, rounded spoonfuls. Return the skillet to very low heat and cook the mounds for 2 minutes. With a slotted spoon or two forks, turn the mounds over and cook for another 2 minutes, or until the meringues are firm to the touch. Transfer to a paper towel and drain. Repeat with the remaining egg whites, again making 3 mounds and cooking and draining them in the same manner. Reserve the milk.

{continued}

laskin floating islands {continued}

—●*

PILE THE MERINGUES in a shallow bowl and chill in the refrigerator.

TO MAKE THE CUSTARD: Strain the reserved milk into a 2-cup measure and add enough fresh milk to make 2 cups.

POUR THE MILK into a double boiler insert. Add the vanilla bean. Heat over boiling water until bubbles appear around the edge of the pan. Remove the insert and lower the heat so the water remains at a simmer.

IN A MEDIUM BOWL, whisk the egg yolks together with the sugar. Slowly stir the egg mixture into the hot milk, stirring constantly. Replace the insert over the bottom of the double boiler and cook the custard over simmering water, stirring constantly, until the mixture thickens and coats the back of a metal spoon, about 8 to 10 minutes.

WHEN THE CUSTARD is thickened, remove the insert and place in a bowl filled with ice cubes to chill the custard quickly, stirring as it chills. When it is cool to the touch, about seven minutes, refrigerate until ready to serve. To serve, place the custard in individual dishes, and top each portion with a meringue. Add a few strawberries or raspberries, if desired.

ingredients

2	TABLESPOONS UNSALTED BUTTER, MELTED
1/2	CUP SEMISWEET MINI-CHOCOLATE CHIPS
1	15-OUNCE CAN PITTED BING CHERRIES, WELL DRAINED
4	LARGE EGGS
1	CUP MILK
3/4	CUP ALL-PURPOSE FLOUR
1	TEASPOON VANILLA EXTRACT
1/2	CUP GRANULATED SUGAR
1/4	TEASPOON GROUND CINNAMON
	CONFECTIONERS' SUGAR FOR DUSTING

*serves 6-8

chocolate-cherry clafouti

THE RECIPE for clafouti originated in the region of Limousin, known for its tiny, tart black cherries. That is why it is traditionally made with cherries, which are topped with a batter, but other fruits can certainly be used. Peaches and the small prune plums of early autumn are tasty choices. Some clafoutis have a puddinglike texture, while others have a more cakelike topping. The dish is served warm, often with a pitcher of heavy cream. This recipe departs from tradition by adding semisweet chocolate, a delicious counterpoint to the flavor of the cherries.

PLACE THE OVEN RACK in the middle position and preheat the oven to 350°F. Brush an 11-x-7-inch baking dish with 1 tablespoon of the butter. Place the chocolate chips in the bottom of the prepared dish and then the cherries.

IN A FOOD PROCESSOR or blender, combine the remaining tablespoon of butter, the eggs, milk, flour, vanilla, granulated sugar, and cinnamon. Process or blend until smooth. Pour the batter carefully over the cherry-chocolate base.

BAKE THE CLAFOUTI for 50 to 55 minutes, until puffed and golden, or a knife inserted near the edge comes out clean. Cool on a baking rack for about 10 minutes. Dust with confectioners' sugar just before serving.

ingredients

1/2 CUP BRANDY

5 MEDIUM PEACHES, PEELED, PITTED, AND SLICED (SEE NOTE)

SOFTENED BUTTER OR VEGETABLE-OIL COOKING SPRAY FOR THE BAKING DISH

5 LARGE EGGS

1 CUP HALF-AND-HALF

1/4 CUP ALL-PURPOSE FLOUR

1/2 CUP GRANULATED SUGAR

2 TABLESPOONS CONFECTIONERS' SUGAR, SIFTED, FOR GARNISH

1/2 CUP TOASTED SLIVERED ALMONDS FOR GARNISH (SEE NOTE)

NOTE: To peel peaches, plunge them into boiling water for 1 minute, and then drain them in a colander. With a paring knife, make an X on the bottom of the peach and then remove the skin sections.

To toast almonds, place them on a baking sheet in a 350°F oven for 6 to 7 minutes, or until golden brown.

almond-peach clafouti la combe

I HAVE BEEN FORTUNATE enough to teach at a lovely eighteenth–century French country house deep in the Périgord region of southwest France. Wendely Harvey and Robert Cave-Rogers, the owners, have restored the buildings beautifully, even beyond their former glory. They open their home to small groups to come and cook and absorb the culture as well as the cuisine of this remarkable corner of France. Nothing is spared to make guests feel special and cosseted. The cooking classes are hands-on, in a wonderfully equipped kitchen. This delicious clafouti, a traditional French dessert made with a custardlike batter poured over fresh fruit, is a sample of *la cuisine de La Combe*.

POUR THE BRANDY into a shallow bowl and add the sliced peaches. Gently stir to coat each slice with the brandy. Set aside while you prepare the batter.

PLACE THE OVEN RACK in the middle position and preheat the oven to 350°F. Butter or spray a 10½-inch round or 11-x-7-inch baking dish.

IN A BLENDER or a food processor, combine the eggs, half-and-half, and flour just until blended. Add the granulated sugar and blend or process until smooth, about 1 minute. Drain the peaches and add the brandy marinade to the batter.

ARRANGE the peach slices in a spiral or close-fitting pattern in the prepared baking dish. Pour the batter carefully over the fruit.

BAKE THE CLAFOUTI until the custard is firm and the top is golden, about 30 to 35 minutes, or until a knife inserted near the edge comes out clean. Transfer to a rack to cool until slightly warm or at room temperature. Sprinkle with confectioners' sugar and toasted almonds and serve.

chocolate-studded foam of zabaglione

ZABAGLIONE, the ethereal, foamy, wine-flavored custard of Italian origin, is taken to a new level in this delectable dessert. Perfectly delicious on its own, zabaglione is sometimes poured over golden pound cake or served over a bowl of fresh fruit. In this recipe, whipped cream makes it even lighter and foamier, and tiny chips of bittersweet chocolate complete the taste sensation. This creation is particularly attractive when served in chilled balloon wine glasses. Be sure to check the label of the Marsala because there is both dry and sweet available, and the labels are similar. I find the sweet too cloying for this dessert. The French version of zabaglione, called sabayon, is made with Cointreau, Tawny Port, or kirsch instead of Marsala.

ingredients

6	LARGE EGG YOLKS
7	TABLESPOONS SUPERFINE SUGAR (SEE PAGE 51)
3/4	CUP DRY MARSALA
2	CUPS HEAVY CREAM
4	OUNCES HIGH-QUALITY BITTERSWEET CHOCOLATE, FINELY CHOPPED

IN THE INSERT of a double boiler, off the heat, whisk together the yolks and the sugar until fluffy and lemon colored. Add the Marsala to the egg-and-sugar mixture, and place the insert over simmering water. Whisk the mixture constantly. It will froth up and then form a soft, foamy mass. The zabaglione is done when the mixture mounds slightly when dropped from a spoon, about 15 to 20 minutes.

REMOVE THE INSERT and pour the zabaglione into a large bowl to cool.

MEANWHILE, in another large bowl, whip the cream with an electric mixer until fairly stiff.

FOLD the whipped cream into the zabaglione, and then gently fold in the chocolate.

POUR into a glass bowl or individual wine glasses and refrigerate for at least 1 hour, or up to 3 hours.

tiramisu cortonese

TIRAMISU is a delightful concoction enjoyed in Italy as I have found on my yearly pilgrimage to Cortona. There are as many versions as there are Americans wandering the piazza, looking for a glimpse of places mentioned in Frances Mayes's novel, *Under the Tuscan Sun*. Look for the true Italian ladyfingers, *Savoiardi*, at an Italian grocery. They make a big difference in the texture of the final dish. Easily doubled, this recipe needs to be chilled at least 6 hours before serving.

MAKE THE ZABAGLIONE up to the point where you remove it from the double boiler and pour it into a bowl to cool. Refrigerate it while you prepare the ladyfingers. Pour the coffee into a pie plate and quickly and gently (in about 10 seconds) dip 2 of the ladyfingers in the espresso. Crumble them into the bottom of a martini or wine glass. Repeat for the remaining 3 glasses.

IN A LARGE MIXING BOWL, gently blend the Zabaglione and the mascarpone cheese together until smooth, and then fold in the whipped cream and cocoa. Spread half the mixture over the ladyfingers in each glass.

TWO AT A TIME, dip the remaining 8 ladyfingers in the remaining espresso, and crumble them on top of the cream mixture in each glass. Spread the remaining Zabaglione mixture over this second layer of ladyfingers, smoothing the top.

COVER THE GLASSES with plastic wrap and refrigerate for at least 6 hours, or preferably overnight. Just before serving, garnish the desserts with the chocolate shavings or a sprinkling of sifted cocoa. If you wish, the Tiramisu may be layered and served from a bowl or platter, or assembled in smaller wine glasses.

ingredients

1 RECIPE ZABAGLIONE (PAGE 94), WITH NO WHIPPED CREAM OR CHOCOLATE ADDED, CHILLED IN A BOWL AND REFRIGERATED

2 CUPS STRONG ESPRESSO COFFEE, COOLED

16 *SAVOIARDI* (ITALIAN LADYFINGERS) OR DOMESTIC LADYFINGERS (SEE NOTE)

8 OUNCES MASCARPONE CHEESE

1/2 CUP HEAVY CREAM, WHIPPED

3 TABLESPOONS UNSWEETENED COCOA, SIFTED

2 OUNCES BITTERSWEET CHOCOLATE, SHAVED WITH A VEGETABLE PEELER, FOR GARNISH (OPTIONAL)

SIFTED COCOA FOR GARNISH (OPTIONAL)

4 10-OUNCE MARTINI OR WINE GLASSES

NOTE: If you are using the softer sponge cake domestic ladyfingers, place them on a baking sheet and toast them in a 375°F oven for 10 minutes.

*makes 1 quart

chocolate-almond frozen custard ice cream

NO CUSTARD COLLECTION would be complete without a bow to custard-based ice cream. This is not the soft custard dispensed by frozen custard machines, but a lush, silky-to-the-tongue confection, a true French style ice cream. When my children were young, ice cream making was a huge treat in the summer. We would follow the fresh fruits of the season in turn. Strawberries came first, then blueberries, raspberries, and finally the juicy peaches of August. Chocolate, however, was always the all-seasons favorite. I've included some fruit-based variations. Be sure to use a high-quality chocolate for this recipe.

IN THE INSERT of a double boiler, heat the milk, ½ cup of the sugar, and the salt over simmering water, stirring frequently to dissolve the sugar. Do not boil. Add the chocolate, stirring until melted.

IN A MEDIUM BOWL, whisk the yolks with the remaining ¼ cup of sugar. Slowly whisk in about ½ cup of the hot chocolate mixture. Then slowly whisk the tempered egg mixture into the chocolate mixture in the double boiler insert. Cook over the simmering water, stirring frequently, until the mixture begins to thicken and coats the back of a metal spoon, about 18 minutes. Strain the mixture through a sieve into a glass or metal bowl, cover the surface with plastic wrap, and refrigerate for at least 2 hours, or even overnight.

WHEN THE MIXTURE is chilled, stir in the heavy cream and almonds. Pour the contents into the chilled canister of your ice-cream maker and freeze according to the manufacturer's directions. Enjoy immediately or pack into a container and freeze.

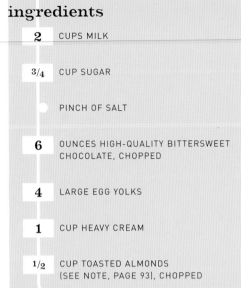

2	CUPS MILK
3/4	CUP SUGAR
●	PINCH OF SALT
6	OUNCES HIGH-QUALITY BITTERSWEET CHOCOLATE, CHOPPED
4	LARGE EGG YOLKS
1	CUP HEAVY CREAM
1/2	CUP TOASTED ALMONDS (SEE NOTE, PAGE 93), CHOPPED

FRUITY VARIATIONS:

Follow the recipe, but omit the chocolate and almonds. After the mixture has chilled, for a richer vanilla flavor, you may add 2 teaspoons of vanilla extract. Then fold in 1 cup of sliced or gently mashed fresh berries or 1 cup of chopped or mashed ripe peaches.

ingredients

✳ custard sauce

3	CUPS HALF-AND-HALF
6	LARGE EGG YOLKS
1/2	CUP SUGAR
1/4	TEASPOON SALT
●	ICE CUBES FOR CHILLING CUSTARD
2	TABLESPOONS LIGHT RUM

✳ trifle

1	1-POUND FROZEN POUND CAKE, THAWED AND CUT INTO ¾-INCH CUBES
1/4	CUP LIGHT RUM
1	CUP PEACH JAM, WARMED
2	BANANAS, PEELED, HALVED LENGTHWISE, AND SLICED
2	MANGOS, PEELED, PITTED, AND CUBED
3	KIWIS, PEELED AND CUBED

{ingredients continued}

✳ serves 12

tropical trifle

A PROPER ENGLISH TRIFLE is a delicious concoction of cake, fruit, preserves, custard sauce, and wine or liqueur. The garnish is traditionally candied fruit, nuts, and whipped cream. Supermarkets now abound with exotic fruits from all over the world, so I've taken the trifle one step further from tradition and included a variety of tropical fruit. Use the recipe as a guideline, and buy whatever fruit looks good in the market. Substitute papaya or peaches for the mango. Another alternative is the tropical fruit mix that comes in 24-ounce plastic jars, available in the canned fruit section of many supermarkets. Drained well, this makes an acceptable substitute.

———✳

TO MAKE THE CUSTARD SAUCE: In a medium saucepan, heat the half-and-half just until steam begins to rise.

IN THE INSERT of a double boiler, combine the yolks, sugar, and salt. Add the half-and-half very slowly to the eggs, stirring constantly. Cook over simmering water, stirring constantly, until the mixture coats the back of a metal spoon, about 6 minutes. Remove the insert and set it in a bowl of ice. Chill the custard, stirring occasionally, and stir in the rum. Lay a sheet of plastic wrap over the surface of the custard and refrigerate it until ready to use.

TO ASSEMBLE THE TRIFLE: Place half of the cake cubes in a trifle bowl or attractive glass serving dish. Sprinkle the cake with 2 tablespoons of the rum and toss. Spoon half of the jam over the cake and spread it as evenly as possible. Top the jam with half of the cooled custard. Place half of the banana slices, half of the mango cubes, and half of the kiwi slices over the custard in one layer.

{continued}

ingredients

✳ topping

2	CUPS HEAVY CREAM
3	TABLESPOONS SUGAR
1	TABLESPOON LIGHT RUM (OPTIONAL)
1/2	CUP TOASTED SHREDDED COCONUT (OPTIONAL, SEE NOTE)

NOTE: To toast coconut, sprinkle shredded, unsweetened coconut on a baking sheet and bake in a 325°F oven for 6 to 10 minutes, stirring 2 or 3 times, until golden. Transfer the coconut to a plate.

tropical trifle {continued}

PUT THE REMAINING cake cubes in a small bowl, and toss them with the remaining 2 tablespoons of rum. Place the cake cubes on the fruit, and spread the remaining jam over the cake cubes. Top with the remaining fruit, and then the remaining custard. Cover and refrigerate for at least 3 hours, or even overnight.

BEFORE SERVING, in a medium bowl, whip the cream and sugar until soft peaks form. Add the rum (if desired) and whip until stiff peaks form. Mound the cream over the trifle and sprinkle the coconut over the top, if using. Serve at once.

syllabub

ALTHOUGH THIS PUDDING isn't custard based, I am so enamored of it that I had to include it in this collection. I first tasted this ethereal concoction in England many years ago, and have since taught it to my cooking classes on many occasions. It dates back to the Middle Ages, when syllabub was originally made with "Sille," a French wine from the Champagne region (or sometimes ale) and milk. The "bub" in the name comes from Old English slang for a bubbly drink. Start the syllabub the day before you plan to serve it, and present it in your prettiest wine glasses for maximum effect. This voluptuous dessert would be enhanced served with a dark chocolate cookie.

ingredients

ZEST OF 2 LEMONS, FINELY GRATED, PLUS LENGTHS OF LEMON ZEST (OPTIONAL, SEE NOTE) FOR GARNISH

$1\frac{1}{4}$ CUPS SWEET CREAM SHERRY OR A LATE-HARVEST RIESLING

3 TABLESPOONS BRANDY

$2\frac{1}{2}$ CUPS HEAVY CREAM

2 LARGE EGG WHITES

$\frac{1}{2}$ CUP SUGAR

NOTE: To obtain strips of the zest for garnish, drag a zester down the lemon lengthwise.

IN A GLASS BOWL, combine the grated zest with the sherry, cover with plastic wrap, and leave to soak overnight.

THE FOLLOWING DAY, strain the sherry through a fine sieve lined with cheesecloth into another small bowl. Add the brandy.

USING AN ELECTRIC MIXER, beat the cream in a large bowl until very stiff peaks form.

BEAT THE EGG WHITES in a small bowl until thick, but not stiff. Fold the egg whites into the heavy cream. Whisk in the sugar. Gently fold in the sherry mixture, 2 or 3 tablespoons at a time.

SPOON the syllabub into 8 tall wine glasses and refrigerate for at least 6 hours. If you wish, before serving, garnish each glass with a couple of lengths of lemon zest.

ingredients

1/2 CUP (1 STICK) UNSALTED BUTTER

5 LARGE EGGS

1 CUP SUGAR

GRATED ZEST AND JUICE FROM 5 SMALL LIMES

2 CUPS HEAVY CREAM

SLIVERS OF LIME FOR GARNISH (OPTIONAL)

*serves 6-8

luscious lime divine

NANCY CHAPMAN, a resident of my town of Center Harbor, New Hampshire, is a talented writer as well as an excellent cook. In her youth, she cooked for one of the families who make their summer homes in this beautiful region of our state. This creamy, cooling dessert was pronounced "Lime Divine" by the lady of the house, and has remained so named ever since. It is beautiful served in parfait or wine glasses, garnished with a sliver of lime.

MELT THE BUTTER in the insert of a double boiler over simmering water.

IN A MEDIUM BOWL, whisk the eggs and sugar together until foamy. In a slow, steady stream, add the melted butter. Transfer the mixture to the double boiler and gently cook, stirring, for 10 minutes, or until slightly thickened. Remove from the heat and gently stir in the lime zest and juice. Transfer the custard to a large bowl and refrigerate until chilled, about 2 hours.

MEANWHILE, in a large bowl, whip the cream until fairly stiff. With a wooden spoon, gently fold the whipped cream into the custard. Cover with plastic wrap and chill at least 4 hours before serving. Garnish with lime slivers just before serving.

ingredients

2 CUPS MILK

1 TABLESPOON UNFLAVORED GELATIN

3 LARGE EGGS, SEPARATED

1/2 CUP GRANULATED SUGAR

1 TABLESPOON ALL-PURPOSE FLOUR

1 CUP ITALIAN MACAROONS, FINELY CHOPPED IN A FOOD PROCESSOR OR BY HAND

VEGETABLE-OIL COOKING SPRAY FOR THE MOLD

1 TEASPOON AMARETTO LIQUEUR

1 CUP HEAVY CREAM

1-2 TEASPOONS SUPERFINE SUGAR (SEE PAGE 51), AS NEEDED

GLACÉED FRUIT OR *MARRONS* FOR GARNISH (OPTIONAL)

1 4- TO 6-CUP RING MOLD

budino di amaretto

serves 6

A BUDINO is an Italian pudding made with those delicious Italian macaroons called *amaretti*. Look for the Lazzaroni brand, which is available at most Italian groceries. If you are unable to find *amaretti*, a good almond macaroon will work. Using a ring mold makes an attractive presentation. You can really gild the lily by filling the center of the unmolded *budino* with glacéed fruit or *marrons* (candied fruits or chestnuts).

POUR THE MILK into a large bowl and sprinkle the gelatin over it. Let stand 20 minutes.

IN A MEDIUM BOWL, combine the egg yolks, granulated sugar, and flour. Whisk until well blended. Stir into the gelatin mixture, mix well, and pour into the insert of a double boiler. Cook the mixture over simmering water until it is thick enough to coat the back of a metal spoon, about 5 to 7 minutes. Add the macaroons and cool for 15 minutes.

REFRIGERATE the mixture until it is syrupy and beginning to set, about 40 to 45 minutes. Lightly spray the ring mold.

MEANWHILE, in a medium bowl, beat the egg whites until stiff, but not dry. When the macaroon-and-gelatin mixture is at the syrupy stage, remove from the refrigerator and fold in the beaten egg whites and the Amaretto. Transfer the mixture to the prepared ring mold and refrigerate for 4 to 6 hours.

JUST BEFORE SERVING, whip the cream until stiff and sweeten to taste with the superfine sugar. To unmold the *budino*, turn it over on the serving platter and cover with a dish towel that has been rinsed in hot water and wrung out. Holding the mold and the platter together, shake gently to unmold. Serve with a dollop of whipped cream on each plate and glacéed fruit or *marrons*, if desired.

index

table of equivalents

The exact equivalents in the following tables have been rounded for convenience.

LIQUID/DRY MEASURES

u.s.	metric
1/4 teaspoon	1.25 milliliters
1/2 teaspoon	2.5 milliliters
1 teaspoon	5 milliliters
1 tablespoon (3 teaspoons)	15 milliliters
1 fluid ounce (2 tablespoons)	30 milliliters
1/4 cup	60 milliliters
1/3 cup	80 milliliters
1/2 cup	120 milliliters
1 cup	240 milliliters
1 pint (2 cups)	480 milliliters
1 quart (4 cups, 32 ounces)	960 milliliters
1 gallon (4 quarts)	3.84 liters
1 ounce (by weight)	28 grams
1 pound	454 grams
2.2 pounds	1 kilogram

OVEN TEMPERATURE

farenheit	celsius	gas
250	120	1/2
275	140	1
300	150	2
325	160	3
350	180	4
375	190	5
400	200	6
425	220	7
450	230	8
475	240	9
500	260	10

LENGTH

u.s.	metric
1/8 inch	3 millimeters
1/4 inch	6 millimeters
1/2 inch	12 millimeters
1 inch	2.5 centimeters